D1321451

HOLY SHIFT!

Moving Your Company Forward to the Future of Work

Dan Michelson

Holy Shift! Moving Your Company Forward to the Future of Work

Published by Worth Books, an imprint of Forefront Books.
Distributed by Simon & Schuster.

Library of Congress Control Number: 2023911360

Print ISBN: 978-1-63763-220-8
E-book ISBN: 978-1-63763-221-5

Cover Design by Emma Michelson
Interior Design by Mary Susan Oleson, BLU Design Concepts

To Kim, Emma, and Ian
for their love and support
and the journey ahead.

In support of caring for
our neighbors in need
in communities all across our country,
all proceeds from *Holy Shift*
will be donated to Feeding America.

Contents

INTRODUCTION
The Opportunity of a Lifetime

"The barn's burnt down.
Now I can see the moon."

Mizuta Masahide
Japanese Poet and Samurai

Everything was perfect. I felt miserable.

Something very big was missing. I spoke to others and I wasn't alone. Everyone felt exactly the same way.

It was January 2022, and the not-so-Great Resignation was in full swing. It was a punch to the gut that took the wind out of every leader who truly cared about their company and their culture. And it furthered the distance that people were already feeling from their company and coworkers.

I had been on a very fortunate ten-year run as the CEO of a high-growth, high-performing healthcare technology company. It was a job that I never thought I would have and it had gone better than I could have ever expected. We had grown our company from fifty to five hundred people and the enterprise value of the business from $30 million to well over $1 billion. We had the highest customer- and employee-satisfaction scores in our industry. And we had just hit our financial targets and paid out a full bonus to everyone on our team for the tenth year in a row, even in the middle of a pandemic.

This was a great business with a happy team and happy customers. I interviewed every candidate we hired and spoke with every customer. My fingerprints on the company were literally everywhere.

But now the thrill was gone, and there was a chill hanging over every day. Something just didn't feel right.

It was time for me to leave.

There was a major change in motion in the workplace of both scale and substance that none of us had ever seen before. For so many, that sense of pride, purpose, connection, and community that all come from work—were gone.

For me, this shift was so confusing, challenging, and compelling that I quit what was once my dream job to try to figure out what was going on and share what I learned with others. And with my children entering the workforce, it was now even more personal for me. It was time for me to help.

Welcome to *Holy Shift!*

The reason this book is called *Holy Shift* is to shout out that we're in the middle of a truly historic moment relative to the changes in how, where, when, and why we work. It's impacting everyone, everywhere and takes a leap of faith to even begin to get your head around it. And the word *shift* is a play on another word that many of us have been screaming out to deal with this moment of massive change that isn't comfortable for any of us.

When this shift hit me, it caused a level of anxiety that

wouldn't go away. But I wasn't alone. Every leader I spoke with felt it, and it was only getting worse every day. I found this frustrating and fascinating. So I decided to dive deep to try to discover a path forward.

I spoke with hundreds of other CEOs and leaders, read every article I could find, and listened to a never-ending stream of podcasts. But the deeper I dove, the more I just kept coming up empty. Everything I came across only added to the long list of failed tactics on how to bring people *back*. What I was searching for was a pragmatic playbook for how to bring people *forward*.

After months and months of coming up with nothing, I finally took a step back to zoom out. And that's when it hit me . . . the realization that what we're living through may be the single biggest and most rapid change in how we work and live in over a century and, quite possibly, ever. There is a very real possibility that, a thousand years from now, people will look back at this moment as a tipping point, a historic and *Holy Shift*.

This is a very big deal, because history has proven that when our work changes, we change as well. It turns out that our work has always been the force of our nature. But because we don't like to change, every big shift in how we work in history has required a major catalyst . . . like a pandemic. In other words, we've been down this road before.

That realization shifted my anxiety about the moment we're in into a level of excitement that we may be experiencing something momentous. But while that historical perspective provided a spark, in order to truly light a fire, I knew that I had to get a ground-level view of what's happening right now.

For this I teamed up with the world's largest association of CEOs to conduct a survey of over 1,600 companies. The headline from our research was that leaders in every company, country, and industry had one thing in common—a crisis of confidence in their company culture.

Our research revealed clear, consistent themes about the frustrations they were feeling, the problems they were trying to solve, and the ideas they were experimenting with in order to find a path forward. But perhaps the most stunning statistic from our study was the scale of change that has already taken place. In only a handful of years, the majority of people in the world could now "go to work" anywhere at any time. For the first time ever, work was no longer defined as a time or place. Think about that.

The catalyst of a pandemic had once again sparked

a monumental change. We're all living history. Shift has happened.

Combining these historical and real-time views helped me to stop screaming "Holy Sh*t!" and fighting against the moment we're in. It's clear that everyone, everywhere, has the same set of challenges. I'm not alone, you're not alone. But more importantly, what struck me and stunned me is what I can now see more clearly—this is truly a once-in-a-lifetime opportunity for leaders to create a *Holy Shift*.

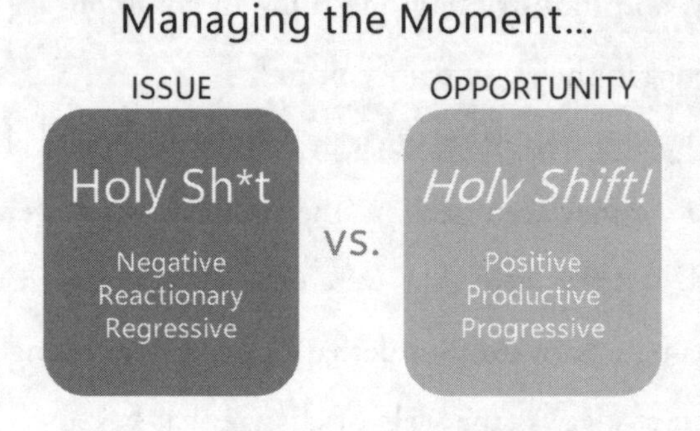

We all have an opportunity to manage this moment in a positive and productive way that can move every company as well as all of us forward into the future.

I had found my epiphany. Finally.

A True Test of Leadership

The chaos and confusion of the last few years has taken its toll. Many people have lost the pride and purpose that comes from work and transitioned into more of a transactional and transitional mindset. The lack of certainty and clarity have caused an enormous level of conflict at all levels of every organization. But those same conditions are now a call to action for all of us who are lucky enough to be leaders. It's an incredible opportunity for all of us to live up to that title.

Leaders are action figures, and perhaps the best action plan comes from an interview that I heard with Dr. Randall Stutman, a recognized expert on executive effectiveness. He was asked for his definition of leadership.[1] His answer was so simple, specific, and spot-on that it shocked me:

"What leaders do is they make situations and people better."

That's exactly right. Leadership isn't about a title; it's about taking action to "make situations and people better." That can come from anyone, anywhere, anytime, and at any level of an organization. This is an exceptional filter to assess whether someone is truly a leader—are they making the people around them and the situations they're in better? This radically simplifies how someone can assess their own effectiveness as a leader as well as the leadership skills of others.

There was a statement that I shared with our company as advice during an emergency all-hands meeting in mid-March of 2020 when the chaos of the pandemic first hit. While it was the most challenging moment in my thirty-year career and in my ten years as a CEO, it was also the most energizing. This is what I shared:

"In times of chaos, confusion, and conflict,
character is revealed, leaders emerge."

The chaos, confusion, and conflict of the last few years has provided a unique opening for leaders to emerge. We need them to help us navigate this brave new world as an opportunity instead of a threat, and to play an active role in making people and situations better. That's a call to action and an action plan for all of us.

This is an opportunity of a lifetime for leaders to lead, but we have to be both practical about the situation we're in and optimistic that we can and will get to a better place. That's where I'm hoping that I can be helpful, as pragmatism and optimism are at the core of who I am. As Theodore Roosevelt once said:

"People don't care how much you know,
until they know how much you care."

But in order to trust me and understand how much I care, I need to be vulnerable enough to let you get to know me. Well, here you go . . .

Pragmatism + Optimism

The quote "the barn's burnt down, now I can see the moon" at the opening of this book is one that I found early in life when I was struggling. My father didn't want to be one. He left our family just before my first birthday. At the time, my mom was an unemployed schoolteacher with two kids and two hundred dollars in her bank account. It was a tough start.

I grew up extraordinarily introverted and reclusive. I was also dyslexic, constantly bullied, and had a crippling level of social anxiety. The remnants of my childhood were that I didn't think too highly of myself or my prospects in life.

But because of this, I learned a few tricks that set the stage for this book and for the shift we all now need to make.

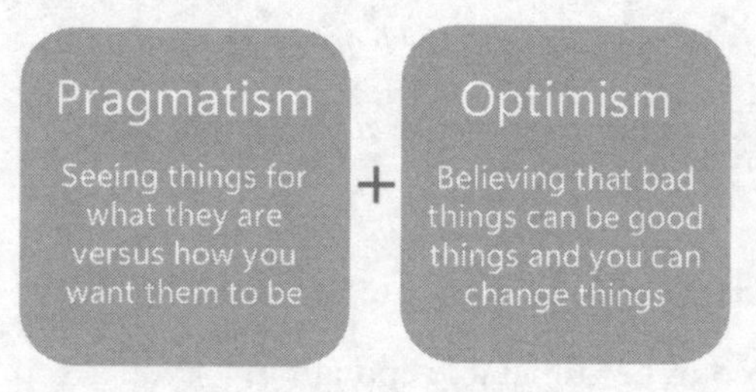

The first trick I learned was to start seeing things as they were versus how I wanted them to be. I learned how to be a *pragmatist.*

Like many children of divorce, I grew up thinking I had done something wrong and it was my fault. This killed my ability to trust anyone for pretty much the first thirty years of my life. My wall started to fall as I began to open my eyes to the obvious. It was 1969 when my father had left; he was a messed-up person and took the same road as many others at that time. And he made some bad choices, including insisting that my mom put us up for adoption, which was the catalyst that set the divorce in motion.

Over time, I began to see this for what it was. It had nothing to do with me; it was all about him. This simple pivot in perspective was an epiphany for me. It taught me to be pragmatic and see things for what they really are. But any strength can also be a weakness. If you only see things as they are, it limits your ability to see things for what they can be.

That leads to the second trick that I learned, which was that bad things can be good things and you can change things. I learned how to be an *optimist*.

My father's leaving opened up the opportunity for my mom to get remarried to a screw salesperson from Fort Wayne, Indiana. I was legally adopted and changed my last name when I was in fourth grade. I had lost a father, but for the first time I had a dad. While we had a hard time connecting with each other when I was growing up, I eventually ended up growing out of my angst and anger. And when I got married, I asked him to be the best man at my wedding because he was the best and most important man in my life. Up until he passed away a few years ago, he was always there for me, always listening.

The experience of losing a father but gaining a dad

helped me understand the difference between the two. And it ended up making me a much more present and caring parent when my wife and I were given the gift of two healthy kids. So, a bad thing turned into a good thing, and it helped change things for me and for my family.

This was my lived experience about the power of optimism. And that's why a simple quote about a barn means so much to me.

When something bad happens, when "the barn's burnt down," you're given the opportunity to see something bigger and even better—in this case, "the moon." If the worst thing that had ever happened to me, a parent abandoning me, ended up bringing me something else that helped shape me, something positive, then there was a reason to believe.

So, pragmatism and optimism. The power of those two perspectives got me through some tough times personally and also became my strengths professionally. And they are exactly why I was able to help create world-class, high-performing cultures at two high-growth companies over the last two decades.

I knew what it was like to be isolated, so I felt a sense of responsibility to help every single person on the team. I had learned to trust no one, so I understood that you have to be vulnerable, because it turns out that trust is something you give, not something you get. I learned in a very personal way that one moment doesn't determine who we are or who we can be, so I recognized the importance of stepping up for other people in their darkest moments. I had lived through a constant feeling of having no place or purpose, so I recognized the power of helping people become part of something bigger than themselves and the deep sense of pride and purpose that can come from being part of a team, community, and company.

In that spirit, pragmatism combined with optimism is

the mindset that I used to help explore the moment we're in and write this book. It's also the frame of mind that anyone can leverage to help their company make a *Holy Shift* forward.

It's time to let go of the past; *the barn has burnt down*. My hope is that what I share in this book will help leaders and those they lead feel like they *can now see the moon*. We all now have an amazing opportunity to build something even better together. Let's get moving.

Hands, Head, and Heart

The purpose of this book is to provide leaders at any and every level of a company or organization with ideas and actions that help address the not-so-easy, very big, and thorny questions that we are all trying to answer: How did we get here, where do we go from here, and how do we get there?

With that said, you can put information in someone's *hands*, but that doesn't mean they'll care about it, understand it, or absorb it. You have to work a little harder to provide context and strive to get it into their *head*. But if you're really going to move the needle to inspire someone to act, you've got to get it into their *heart*. In that spirit, I poured my heart into this book with the hope that it hits that same space for you.

Holy Shift will take you and your team to the heart of the matter. It combines *reflection* of how we got to now, *research* on what leaders and companies have set in motion, and a *roadmap* to the future in the form of a strategic framework and practical playbook. While I would love for you to read it from cover to cover, I would encourage you to jump ahead to the parts that are most pressing. Most leaders are stuck in neutral at the moment, so the book is mapped into three simple steps that you can take right now to create momentum to move your company forward to the future of work.

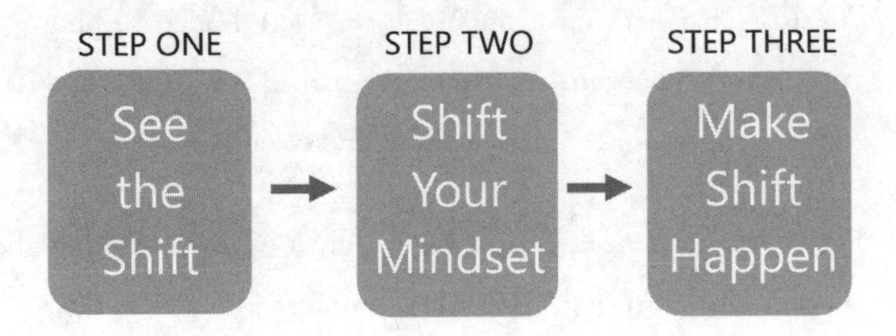

STEP ONE: See the Shift — What we're living through may be the single biggest and fastest shift in how we work and live in history. In other words, shift has happened. Understanding how we got to now will help us to determine where we should go from here.

STEP TWO: Shift Your Mindset — Shifts in thinking are now needed to help you turn culture into a strategy for your company. It's time to pivot from a tactical focus of bringing people *back*, to a strategic focus that brings people *together*.

STEP THREE: Make Shift Happen — Here's your strategic framework and practical playbook to make shift happen. The focus is on what's most important for every leader; helping people on your team feel like they're part of the CORE and connected to your company, culture, and coworkers.

The good news is that this is truly a once-in-a-lifetime opportunity to turn a "Holy Sh*t" moment into a *Holy Shift* movement for you and your company.

It's time to move forward.

Welcome to *Holy Shift*.

STEP ONE
See the Shift

"The more you know about the past,the better you are prepared for the future."

Theodore Roosevelt
26TH PRESIDENT OF THE US

In order to both understand and get through any challenge, it's helpful to zoom out to see if we've faced something similar in the past. This incredibly practical concept applies to anything we have to work through personally, as well as things we're forced to deal with collectively. It can be a great opportunity, or a missed opportunity, to take some lessons learned from yesterday and apply them to today.

In that spirit, one of the best ways to address the problems in the workplace right now is to take a step back to learn from pivots that have happened in the past. It turns out that pandemics have had a funny little habit—make that a not-so-funny, painful, very big habit—of changing both how we work and live in a very big way. The better we understand that context of the historical shifts that we're experiencing in our professional and personal lives, the bigger the potential. Moments like this are truly a gift if you're trying to drive change and move your company forward, but only if you can overcome the inertia that's holding you back.

Overcoming Inertia

The ability to overcome inertia is perhaps the most important attribute and tangible output of any leader. This law of physics,

Newton's First Law of Motion, is that objects in motion tend to stay in motion, unless acted upon by an opposing force.

Overcoming Inertia at Work

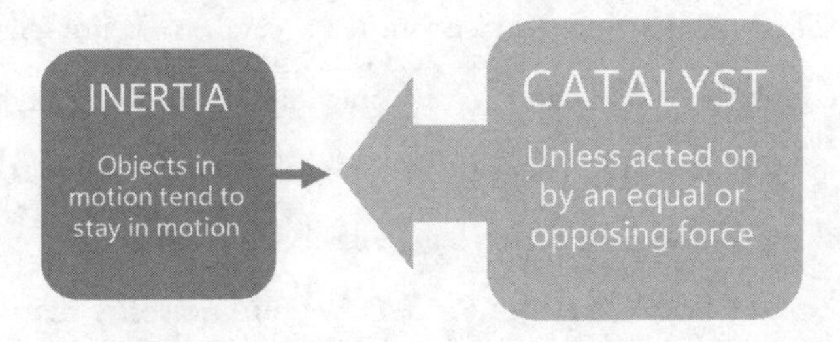

In the context of a business, inertia refers to a company's tendency to stay the same, even in the face of changing circumstances or conditions. This complacency and resistance to change leads to a lack of growth and innovation. Once again, the only thing that a leader needs to overcome this is an equal or opposing force. In that light, what they need the most is a catalyst.

A catalyst that can move a company in a new direction can come in the form of a change in technology, regulations, competition, customer preferences, or even a major event like the one we just went through. The importance of a catalyst in overcoming inertia is that it creates a sense of urgency for change—a "burning platform." In that sense, a catalyst is a leader's best friend as it inspires action and gives you traction to transform your company's strategy, operations, or even your culture.

In the context of the workplace, we are used to doing things a certain way; we have our habits, and they're hard to break. But when you encounter a catalyst, major change becomes possible—and often inevitable. And throughout history, it turns out that one of the most effective catalysts for such rapid and disruptive change has been pandemics.

In *STEP ONE: See the Shift* we outline shifts that have surfaced in the past, the catalyst for change we've all now been given, and the shocks to the system that put us on a path to move forward from here:

- **A Quick History of How Work Works:** When you zoom out you begin to see that it's possible we're living through the biggest, fastest change in how we work and live in human history. It follows that there will be both new challenges to work through and new opportunities to drive change in ways that wouldn't have been possible otherwise.

- **A Tale of Two Pandemics:** The tale of two pandemics—the Bubonic Plague and the Spanish Flu—reveals a predictable pattern as well as lessons for every leader. In both cases, pandemics drove a stunningly radical transformation in how we work and live. In the aftermath, some leaders fought to bring things back to where they were before, while others were able to recognize and take advantage of the forces at play to jump ahead and drive change. Understanding the tale of these two pandemics provides a perspective that those same opportunities exist for all of us right now.

- **Our Collective Catalyst:** Whether we wanted a catalyst or not, we got one, all of us at the exact same moment. The biggest experiment in the history of work was launched, and companies responded swiftly and effectively. But the aftershock led to a number of side effects, including the collapse of company culture. The good news is that every company is going through it, so we can learn from other leaders and leverage their lessons.

- **The Three Big Shocks to Our System:** There are three seismic shocks to the system that are changing both how we work and live. Understanding these shocks is essential in order to craft and refine a strategy for your company.

It will be critical for leaders to embrace these changes and challenges. We will discuss how to leverage the force of the flow, the power of flex, and the energy of individuals to move your company forward.

Seeing the shift, embracing it as a catalyst, and leveraging the shocks to the system will help you and your company make the most of this moment. A good place to start is with the one pattern that has been in place for millions of years—how and where we *work* has always driven and determined how and where we *live*.

Until now.

CHAPTER ONE
A Quick History of How Work Works

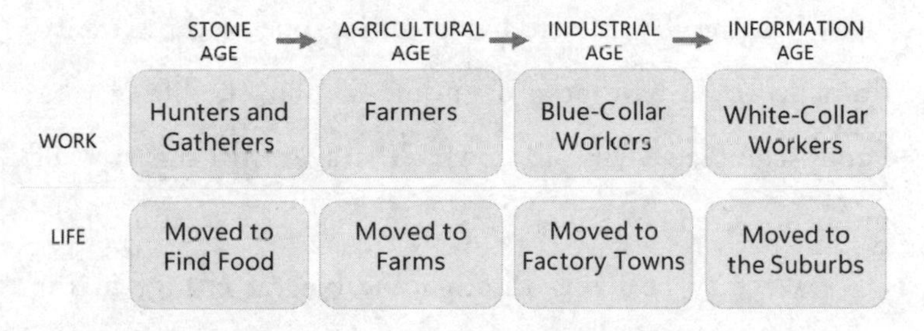

For millions of years our lives have been physically and emotionally centered around our work. Work has been the single biggest force of our nature. We have defined ourselves by our work and spent most of our waking hours working.

Throughout history, the major shifts in where we work have always radically reshaped our lives. Here's a quick 2.5-million-year summary:

- In the Stone Age, we were hunters and gatherers and would move to wherever we could find food.
- In the Agricultural Age, we settled our families on farms where we worked and lived.
- In the Manufacturing Age, people moved to cities and worked in factories.
- In the Information Age, many migrated to the suburbs and worked in offices.

Imagine if you were living during one of those transitions. It would have been daunting, turning the life of your family completely upside down. That's exactly the type of moment we're in.

We may be living through the biggest change in the shortest amount of time in how the workplace works in human history. It's certainly the single biggest change relative to how work fits into and affects people's lives since we transitioned from an agrarian to an industrial economy over a century ago.

From Farms to Factories

The last pivot in how we work and live of this scale and substance was in the early 1900s as we shifted from working and living on farms in rural areas to working in factories and living in cities. This recentered people's lives both personally and professionally in profound ways. Up until the early twentieth century, people had primarily worked on farms and lived in rural communities for over a thousand years.

The shift from the Agricultural Age didn't happen overnight. It was twenty-five hundred years in the making. The transition from farms didn't really start to take hold until the 1700s and 1800s when manufacturing and mass production started to redefine how we work and live in what came to be known as the Industrial Age. Better wages and living standards sparked a slow migration to cities. But the number of people working in factories in this country didn't actually exceed the number of people working on farms until 1920.[2] So, in many ways, this is a relatively recent change.

It's important to understand that this wasn't just a change in where and how people *work* but in where and how they *live*. Shift had happened and it had changed everything.

Factory-Mode Becomes the Model

For the last century, the dominant model of work has been structured around going to and living near a physical location to get work done. Let's refer to that as *Factory-Mode.* During the Industrial Age, people's lives revolved around the factory, which, unlike a farm, was usually far away from their family. In a similar fashion, during the Information Age, our lives have been anchored to an office and often even farther away from our families.

The same model that was created to accommodate the need for physical labor in factories, starting with sweatshops and evolving into manufacturing lines, eventually expanded to include knowledge workers in offices, initially with cubicles and eventually open-office layouts. Advances in roads and public transportation provided the ability for people to move to the suburbs and commute to work. So, the definition and distance of a "company town" expanded, but it was still the same basic proposition and expectation that you need to set up your personal and family life in close proximity to your professional life.

It's absolutely critical to understand that, up until recently, the overall workflow and management approach in offices remained a remnant of how factories were set up over a century ago. You were told what time you needed to show up, take a break, and go home. Your manager was right next to you looking over your shoulder to oversee and review your work, determine your compensation, and promote or fire you if they desired. Senior management set the overall benefits and working conditions. In exchange, you moved to somewhere near where your job was located, spent your personal time commuting to work, contributed to the goals of the company, and were paid for your efforts. And, of course, there was an ongoing tug-of-war over compensation, working conditions, and benefits. So, while at first working in a factory may appear to be very different than working in an office, they have actually been run in pretty much the same Factory-Mode fashion.

This mode has been our model for work and the force of our nature, both personally and professionally, for more than a century. Now suddenly, everything is changing. But is it possible that the tension of the transition we're now going through was somewhat predictable? It turns out we may not be as unique as we think.

CHAPTER TWO

A Tale of Two Pandemics

A Tale of Two Pandemics	ONE Bubonic Plague 1347–1352 (estimate)	TWO Spanish Flu 1918–1919 (estimate)
Increased Wages	✓	✓
Improved Work Conditions	✓	✓
Enhanced Job Mobility	✓	✓

WHILE THE CHANGES in motion in the workplace may seem completely unprecedented, when you zoom out you can see that we've been here before. It turns out that there are two nearly carbon-copy examples of the profound impact, both good and bad, that pandemics have had on how we work and live. There's a pattern and there's something we can learn from it.

We're all familiar with the opening line to Charles

Dickens's *A Tale of Two Cities*, "It was the best of times, it was the worst of times." Dickens used this opening to set the stage for his story of two towns, but let's instead consider it as the progression of the stages in our Tale of Two Pandemics. At the beginning of each, it was certainly the worst of times; people were scared and felt nothing but darkness and despair. At the same time, out of each of these pandemics came the best of times for driving change in an unprecedented fashion.

The first pandemic sparked the first labor movement and inspired an age of innovation in the form of the Renaissance. The second pandemic also drove major changes in the workplace and sparked the roller-coaster ride of the roaring '20s.

Taken together, the tale of these two pandemics reveals a predictable pattern relative to sparking stunning transformations in how we work and live. They each resulted in a strikingly similar set of changes in the workplace, including better working conditions, higher wages, and enhanced job mobility. And while there was tension around these changes at the time, as there is today, leaders who were able to recognize the forces at play were able to jump ahead. Understanding this Tale of Two Pandemics can help us take advantage of the opportunity to shape the path forward.

Pandemic One: The Bubonic Page

The Bubonic Plague hit between 1347 to 1351. It killed one out of every two people in Europe, and close to 200 million across the world.[3] The scale is stunning; it's just impossible to process the horrifying human toll of this pandemic. So, let's instead pivot to something way less important but central to why you're reading this book: the huge impact that the plague had on the way in which we work.

The business headline from the Bubonic Plague is that it sparked the world's first major labor movement. This is a huge point to understand, as it draws a bridge to what we're experiencing right here and now. Simply stated, because so many people had died and those who survived were scared to go back to work, there weren't enough serfs to work the fields and serve their lords. The aftermath of the human crisis was an economic crisis. Sound familiar?

Sensing the opportunity, peasants demanded wage increases and, if they didn't receive them, started to move to other opportunities. The average wage increase at that time was close to 300 percent.[4] You read that right. It certainly makes any recent wage increases look like a speed bump by comparison. But what was even more shocking is that people whose families were bound to the land of their lords for centuries, now for the first time had the freedom to find new jobs and build a new life. Leaders, otherwise known as landowners, reacted with rage, froze compensation, and put laws in place to make it difficult if not impossible for workers to leave their jobs. They were essentially trying to *bring their people back* to where they were in the pre-pandemic days. So a robust labor market with skyrocketing compensation resulted in a bidding war for talent, while management tried to bring things back to the past. Doesn't that sound familiar as well?

At the same time, this turbulence and tension, as well as newfound freedoms, led to what came to be known as the Renaissance, an age of artistic, spiritual, and individual expression. The world we are in today was dramatically altered by the innovations that came out of that time period. It was a tragedy of epic proportions that led to major technological advancements in education, such as the printing press; in science, including eyeglasses and microscopes; and in architecture, with the large-scale production of iron to support and scale buildings.

Perhaps not as important, but certainly worth a mention: whisky in Scotland, bottled beer in London, and champagne in

France were also invented during this time. All of those turned out to be essential for many of us a few hundred years later in helping us get through our most recent pandemic. The same was true during the Spanish Flu. Not just the need for alcohol and sedation but, more importantly, the impact that another pandemic had on work and innovation.

Pandemic Two: The Spanish Flu

A more recent example of the stunning shift that comes from a pandemic was from one hundred years ago, between 1918 and 1921—the Spanish Flu. It took an estimated 50 million lives, one out of every thirty-six people in the world and more than all twentieth-century wars combined.[5] Another stunning number of lives lost that is difficult to get your head around. But the one outcome that was strikingly similar to the Bubonic Plague, as well as to what we've been through recently, was the impact that the Spanish Flu had on the workplace.

The devastation of the Spanish Flu pandemic, coupled with the culmination of World War I, caused a severe labor shortage, leading to another major labor movement. Comparing pre- and post-pandemic compensation, wages on average increased by over 200 percent across all sectors of the economy.[6] This, again, makes the average 5 percent increase in wages that we saw during our most recent pandemic look relatively small by comparison.

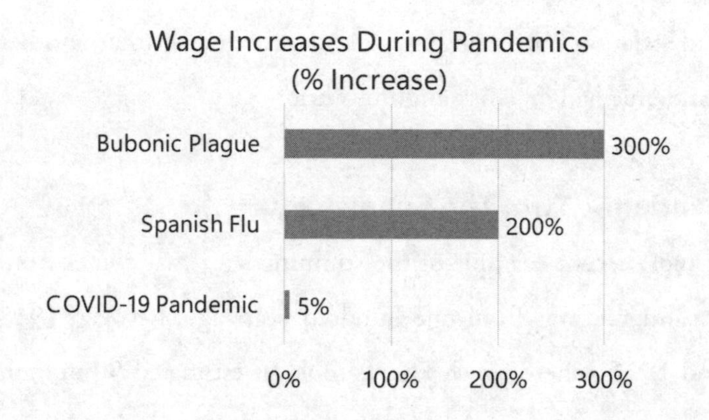

The disproportionate death toll of the flu on men, primarily driven by the close quarters they kept during World War I, and the overall labor shortage driven by the Spanish Flu, resulted in over 25 percent more women joining the workforce.[7] This ultimately led to better access for women relative to the types of industries they could work in as well as the jobs and roles they could take on. In fact, the first female US governor, Nellie Taylor Ross of Wyoming, took office during this time.

There were other changes happening at the time relative to workers' rights, but the strikes and lockouts that accompanied this progress took a toll on the relationships and the level of trust between those in management and those who worked for them. At the time, the collective feeling was that the health of the workplace was in critical condition.

So, another pandemic with another set of big shifts in the workplace, combined with completely different perspectives between labor and management on whether the changes were good or bad. Two pandemics, two-for-two in terms of making massive changes, first on farms and then in factories.

The key for leaders is to recognize that this pattern exists and to realize that moments like this are a once-in-a-lifetime catalyst for change. And if you're given one, it's truly a gift in the form of the chance to try something new.

CHAPTER THREE
Our Collective Catalyst

"Never let a good crisis go to waste."

Sir Winston Churchill
62ND AND 64TH PRIME MINISTER OF THE UK

HUNDREDS IF NOT THOUSANDS of years from now, people will look back to the year 2020 as a historical pivot point in how we work and live. Our worldwide catalyst for change came to us collectively on March 11, 2020, when the headline hit that Rudy Gobert, a center for the Utah Jazz, had COVID-19 and the NBA had cancelled every basketball game and emptied every arena across the country. A few hours later, Tom Hanks, the two-time Academy Award–winning actor, sent out a video sharing that he was just diagnosed. It was the moment that reality hit. Our lives would never be the same. Neither would our work.

The lightning strike of a pandemic forced us to break away from Factory-Mode. Instantly we were all able to prove that the old model, where work only happens if and when you see it happen, was wrong. Businesses reacted swiftly, closing offices, and moving to a remote, virtual approach. Changes that many thought would take decades were deployed overnight. Born out of necessity, the pivot was celebrated as heroic in the capabilities and efficiencies that it brought to companies. While everyone was experiencing fear, the one thing that became clear is that we had collectively figured out a way to keep things moving forward.

In the spirit of Churchill's advice that we should "never let a good crisis go to waste," it was clear that we weren't wasting the opportunity to make major changes.

The Biggest Experiment in the History of Work . . . Worked

Over the next few years, we all participated in a worldwide work experiment of unprecedented size, scope, and scale. Together we accomplished some truly amazing things. What was once unimaginable was now happening everywhere, including within my own company:

- You could set up customer support in someone's kitchen instead of a call center; we did, and our customer service ratings went up.
- You could hire people without ever meeting them in person; we hired and onboarded over one hundred people in the first year of the pandemic.
- You could acquire another company without ever getting together in person; we completed a major acquisition at the height of the pandemic and then achieved three times our first-year sales target without ever meeting anyone in person.
- You could host customer conferences for thousands of people without paying for any space, any food, or anything else; we hosted a virtual conference with over one thousand attendees and had extraordinary ratings.
- You could run very large businesses without any office space; we did it for more than two years even though we had two expensive floors of space sitting vacant.

To be clear, I am not saying that any of these are a better way of doing anything. Some are better; some are worse; most are a little bit of both. The point is that each of those pivots was unimaginable prior to the pandemic, and all of them would be considered unremarkable moving forward.

But while many things got better initially, it turns out that the experiment had some major side effects. Nobody was feeling very well, including me.

The Collapse of Company Culture

To the extent that March 2020 was the moment when companies rose to the occasion, January 2022 was when it felt like we all fell on our faces. It certainly did for me personally and it really hurt.

After a decade of grinding, with the goal of creating an extraordinary company culture, I felt like I had finally hit the target. But then, suddenly, everything that I had built up over those ten years came crashing down in ten days.

At the beginning of the year, our company had hit the peak of Glassdoor, one of the definitive standards in measuring employee experience. We had one of the highest scores in the world for midsize companies. It was a moment I had been working toward for most of my career. I had been obsessed with building and nurturing a caring and compassionate company for over two decades. First, for over ten years as the Chief Marketing Officer of a five-thousand-person public company, and then for the last ten years as the CEO of a five-hundred-person private company. I honestly felt that this was my real purpose, to create a thriving culture that helped people on our team grow and delivered an exceptional customer experience. It's a pretty simple approach, but also pretty effective.

The Simplicity of "Serve"

Every high-performing, built-to-last company that I admired focused on one simple formula—serving their team and serving their customers. And that same approach that I learned from others worked in my time as CEO. We had a ten-year run with the highest employee and customer satisfaction in our industry, leading to a decade-long run of hitting our financial targets and becoming a gold standard in our industry.

I spent half my time as CEO hyper-focused on building a company where everyone felt accepted and respected. I personally interviewed everyone we hired in order to keep a finger on the true pulse of our culture. I also did an exit interview with everyone who left to ensure they knew we appreciated their work. The combination of the many things that we set in motion to build a world-class company culture worked. We had the internal and external surveys and requisite awards in our industry, in our city, and nationally to prove that we were doing something pretty special.

When the pandemic hit, our team couldn't have been more appreciative of our response. We instantly closed our office and assured our team that no one would lose their job or take a pay cut. Twenty-four hours into the pandemic, we made these commitments—and we delivered on every one of them. Our employee engagement hit an all-time high, and we weren't alone; the same was true at many companies.

But as the pandemic stretched out over the course of the next two years, I learned the hard way that you just can't have a thriving culture when people aren't together. As time passed, the remnants of every culture, including ours, were still somewhat present but were no longer prominent. The not-so-surprising reality is that without some level of in-person interaction, the sense of connection between members of a team begins to wither and die.

The definitive turning point was the "not so Great Resignation." At that moment, what was happening in the market relative to compensation was going to lead to some extraordinarily challenging conversations. While we were the poster child for transparency, briefing everyone in our company that this force of nature would affect every business and organization, not just ours, we still got pummeled. Exploding consumer demand driven by pandemic funding and unfettered access to capital had turbocharged the labor market, with a flood of people leaving every company for raises of anywhere from five to 50 percent after a ten-minute search. And why wouldn't they leave when, in reality, they weren't leaving a job but just logging in to another website? Culture was being eaten by compensation because culture had left the table; it wasn't in the building anymore—nobody was.

Those exits left behind one big side effect for everyone else, a feeling that they weren't being treated fairly. People concluded that if another company was giving folks more, then we must be underpaying our team. We had just given the largest raises in the history of our company, well above our peers and benchmarks, but it didn't matter. We couldn't fight this feeling. Not only were people leaving, which was hard enough, but the people who stayed felt incredibly frustrated.

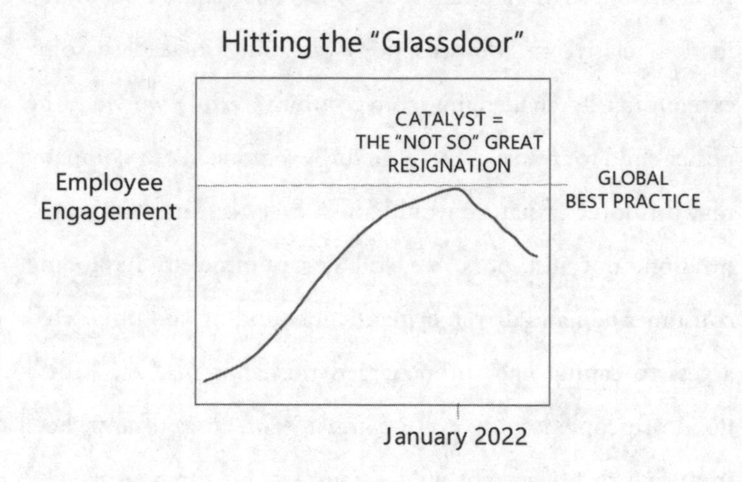

After a decade of hard work to build up to the peak of Glassdoor, our rating plummeted, and we began a nosedive into mediocrity in a matter of days. Even though I knew it was just a reflection of the moment that all companies were in, I would be lying if I said I didn't take it personally. It was brutal, and it bothered me deeply. After over thirty years of working, for the first time in my professional career I was feeling a complete lack of purpose. If no one cared about the company, then why should I? I knew this wasn't the case, but it certainly felt that way. Without the personal touch, I felt out of touch. Not just out of touch with other people, but also with myself. It turns out that I wasn't alone.

One of the clear, consistent trends across every company is that while the pandemic pulled us all together initially, it eventually pulled us apart. Simply stated, COVID killed culture at every company, including ours. The good news is we can commiserate with and learn from many others as this is something we are going through globally. So let's take a look at what in the world has been going on.

Every CEO Has the Same Problem in Common

To better understand the actions that leaders are taking and the plays they are setting in motion, I reached out to YPO, the largest global community of CEOs in the world with 33,000 members. Together we created and conducted a survey of 1,681 chief executives from across 96 countries and more than 47 industries.[8] This representative sample provided insight into how CEOs across the world felt about how the workplace was changing as well as the actions they were taking to move forward.

Our research revealed that the shift in how we work was causing a very real rift between leaders and the people on their team. But, contrary to the narrative, the reason CEOs wanted to get folks back to the office wasn't because they were worried about productivity. It was that they were trying to solve the one problem that every company now has in common—a crisis of confidence in company culture.

A Crisis of Confidence in Company Culture

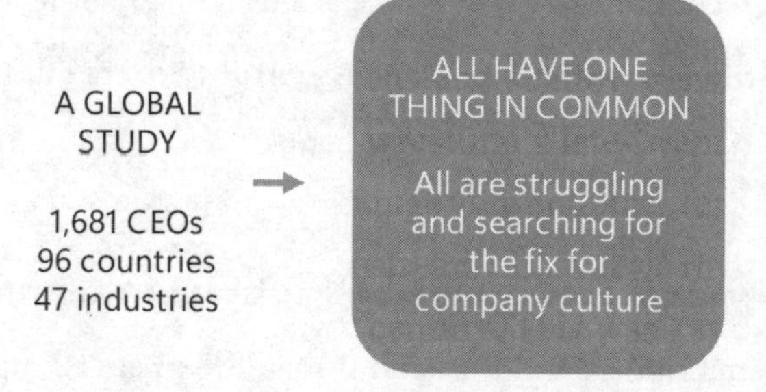

Their primary concern was related to the overall experience and long-term growth and development of their employees. They were worried that their people weren't getting the experiences they needed or building the relationships necessary to grow. It was clear that CEOs were confident they could run their companies effectively in the short-term. But they were very concerned that the crisis in company culture was going to significantly impact performance in the long term.

Many leaders are struggling to find the way forward. They have set many things in motion, including creating more flexible approaches, prioritizing employee development, investing in tools and technologies to improve employee experience, and making mental health a top priority. The problem is that, while all of these efforts are well-intentioned, nothing is hitting the mark. CEOs everywhere still feel that their company culture has collapsed, and they're all trying to find the fix.

Leaders have found that the solution isn't simply to bring people back to the office. But if that's not the answer, what is? It all starts with recognizing that things have changed and then finding ways to leverage the momentum of the moment, instead of fighting against it. If only there was a data point that could point them in the right direction . . . well, it turns out there is.

According to our research and consistent with many other studies, the primary workspace for more than half of the people on the planet is now their home. This has tripled over the last three years, from 18 percent of people pre-pandemic to 54 percent post-pandemic. This figure includes people who work remotely as well as those who work in a hybrid setting.

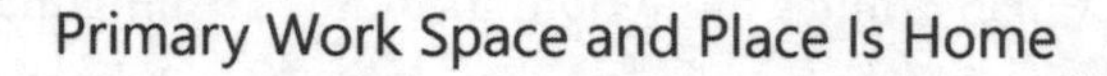

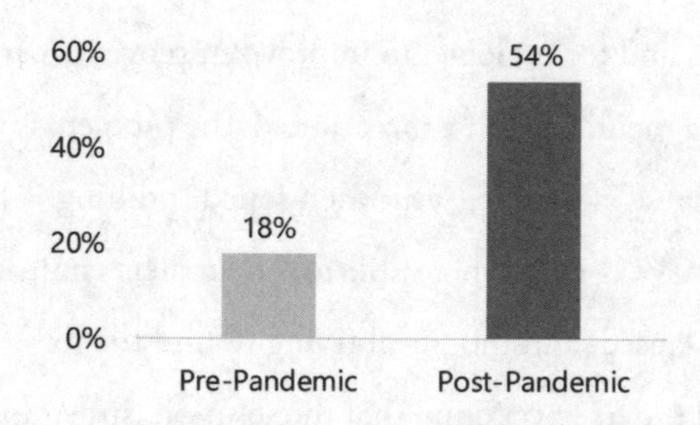

To be clear, close to half of the people in the world no longer have to "go to work" in order to work. That size of a shift in such a short time frame makes this the biggest and fastest recentering of our lives in history. Not surprisingly, it is a pretty big adjustment for everybody, not just professionally, but personally.

While some view this data point as the problem, understanding its implications actually turns out to be the answer. A shift has happened, and it's time to understand it and embrace it, both the issues and the opportunities. Think of it as having been given the biggest gift you could ever receive in terms of a catalyst for change. This new world has opened up a whole new universe of possibilities relative to scaling a company, sourcing talent, getting work done, driving efficiency, and creating a potentially better balance for everyone, including senior management. The list goes on and on. At the same time, it has also brought with it a number of challenges that are all centered around how we experience work, both individually and collectively. That's the problem to solve, and that's where our focus should be.

To that end, in the next chapter we'll outline the three aftershocks that came from the catalyst. This will help you to better inform, craft, and refine a strategy for your company. As we say in software, these are "features" not "bugs" of what is now the modern workplace. Seeing these *shocks to the system* for what they are will help you and your company make the most of this moment.

CHAPTER FOUR

The Three Big Shocks to Our System

Shocks to Our System

SHOCK #1	Workflow Your Life Revolves Around Work	→	LIFEFLOW It All Flows Together
SHOCK #2	Factory-Mode Work Is a Specific Time and Place	→	FLEX-MODE Work Is Fluid and Flexible
SHOCK #3	Collective Concept All Together All the Time	→	INDIVIDUAL EXPERIENCE Me and My Team

The most important thing for leaders to recognize is what has always been true: when our work changes, *we* change. And when shift happens, we need to avoid fighting against the force of those changes and instead leverage their momentum to move us forward. As the Franz Kafka quote goes,

"In man's struggle against the world, bet on the world."[9]

All leaders want to make sure that they're not on the wrong side of that bet. While leaders talk publicly about the need for people in their company to change, many also complain privately that people on their team don't embrace it. So it's ironic that we've just experienced the biggest and fastest change in how we work that we'll ever see, and it's the folks on the senior team who are fighting against it. To be clear, that's exactly how I felt when I was in the CEO seat and would walk through the two floors of our expensive office space and see empty chairs day after day. So I get it, both the anxiety and the anger that leaders may feel. But I've now come to accept that these changes are a permanent part of our lives, and fighting against them is a losing battle and a bad bet. The good news is that we can leverage the force, power, and energy of these changes in the workplace to propel your company forward.

So, let's take a closer look at the three shocks to the system and their impact on how we work and live. The first is the move away from our lives being physically tethered to where we work; the second is the movement to a less-structured approach called Flex-Mode; and the third is the shift from work being a collective concept to more of an individual experience. Let's start with the first, the shift from Workflow to Lifeflow.

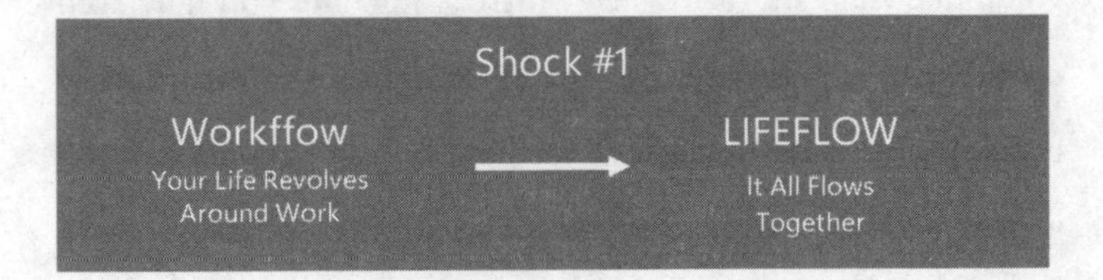

There's an old quote that I wrote down on a piece of paper and carried around for over twenty years:

"As the river flows, the river goes."

While I imagine this may appear mundane to many, it resonated with and changed me. I had always been someone who swam upstream, making things much more difficult than they needed to be. Because of some of the challenges I experienced growing up, I was angry, argumentative, and always fighting against the current. But over time I learned that when you took a step back to understand the true nature of something, you could find a way to swim downstream and go with the flow.

The concept of flow is that once you recognize the natural direction of something, you can leverage it more effectively. While you can try to swim upstream, it's really hard, you'll likely fall short of where you're going, and you may even drown. On the other hand, if you recognize the direction of the flow and swim downstream, it's really easy, incredibly energizing, and you can harness the power of the current to swim fast and far.

For leaders and companies, that perspective provides the path and a prompt to take a step back and recognize how our work and our lives now flow. The best employers will be the ones who help ensure that your job fits into your life, instead of asking you to set your life aside for your work. Things have shifted from *Workflow* to *Lifeflow*. And that's a massive shock to our system because work has always been our flow.

Where We Go Is Our Flow

We've all heard the expression "we're creatures of habit," but stop for a moment and really think about what that means.

Habits aren't just what we do, they end up creating who we are. In that light, we are our habits—and our work has been perhaps our biggest habit of all. We spend most of our waking hours at work for most of our adult life. Work isn't just *a* force of nature; it is *the* force of our nature.

The flow of our lives has always been physically centered around work. Let's refer to that reality as *Workflow*. While where we go to work has always been the dominant force, over time, humans have adapted out of necessity. And when our work changes, we change. Research suggests that it takes sixty-six days to form a new habit.[10] Now that we're well over one thousand days past the start of the last pandemic, it's safe to say that the new habits we formed have changed not just what we do, but who we are.

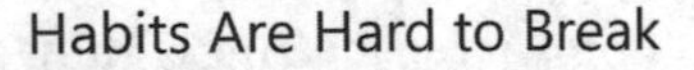

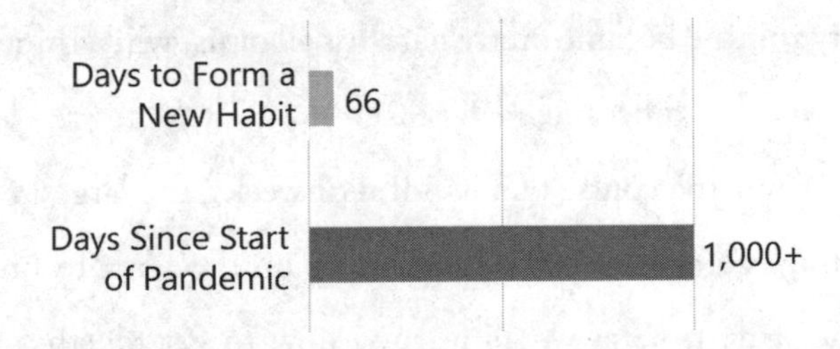

We told people to go virtual and work remotely, and they made the shift. We changed the flow, and people adapted. At our company, productivity increased and we were able to complete hundreds of software implementations without ever going on-site. Our customer satisfaction actually improved, and many companies had similar breakthroughs. Again, I'm not saying this is a better way of doing things, only that we, and many other companies, certainly proved it was viable.

But there were aftershocks in the aftermath of these changes. Going back to the old way of doing things became really hard. Because they were forced to, not because they chose to, people had broken old habits like waking up early, getting ready for work, heading out every morning for a long commute, buying their lunch, getting home late after work, and traveling out of town for meetings. Things that were once pretty routine became pretty hard for all of us, while things that were once hard became really easy.

Over the course of a handful of weeks, the largest group-training exercise in history took place on the same technology at the same time as we all learned how to get together virtually. The endless and exhausting hours of staring at the screen sometimes made us all want to scream, but no one questioned the convenience. And at the end of the experiment, we had learned a new skill, and it got reinforced, over and over and over again, into a new habit. Virtual video calls and meetings replaced e-mail as the work technology that people complain the most about—but can't live without.

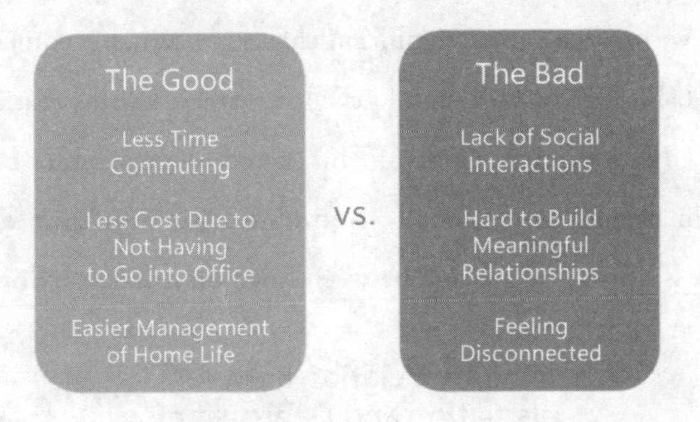

But while people got used to new ways of doing things and being away from others at work, it came at a cost and took a toll.

What people value the most about working from home is not surprising: less time commuting, lower cost by not having to go to an office, and easier management of their home life—all confirmed by a 2022 survey of over 35,000 workers by

Willis Towers Watson.[11] At the same time, the three biggest drawbacks all related to connecting with others: a lack of social interactions, a feeling of being disconnected, and the challenge of building meaningful relationships. That's now the problem to solve, and the root cause is isolation.

The Isolation Epidemic

While the workforce adapted in a stunningly quick and effective way, we now have some significant challenges. When it comes to new habits, the most harmful new one that we have is isolation.

This isolation epidemic hit people pretty hard, both personally and professionally. And it's dangerous to ignore, as there is a direct correlation between isolation and depression in

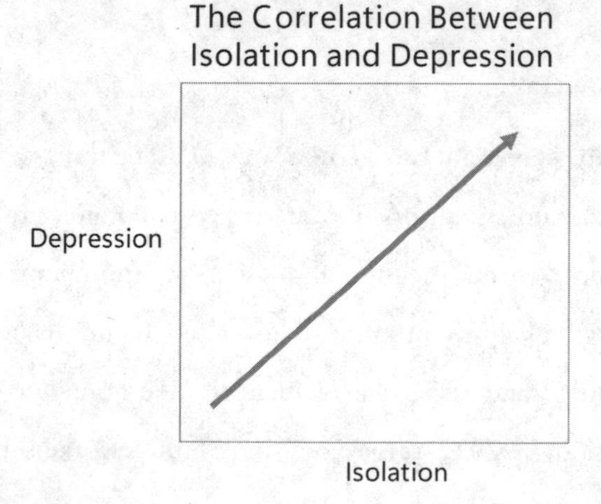

all age groups and in all settings, whether it is a student in high school, a resident in a retirement community, or an individual in the workplace.[12]

While changes in how we work have brought a level of flexibility that has benefited people personally, the level of isolation and lack of social interaction is now the central issue. To be clear, this is a problem for remote companies as well as for hybrid and on-site companies where most people work in a spread-out, distributed fashion. Driving a sense of personal connection between members of your team is now mission critical and a call to action for every company.

Creating that connection is going to be tricky, because while people are more tethered to the workplace than ever, they have never been more distant from their coworkers. There is an opportunity to help address the issue of isolation by communicating the need to create connections within your company. It is essential to not only our professional lives, but also our personal lives. To make this happen, all you need to do is follow the flow.

Go with the Flow

For the first time, we no longer lead separate personal and

professional lives; they are now intertwined. We've transitioned from *Workflow* to something very different—*Lifeflow*.

Lifeflow is a new term and concept that I developed to help companies clear away some of the clutter. For many years, we have used the term *work-life balance*, but it has always been off the mark. The concept that our "life" only exists outside of "work" doesn't reflect our lived experience. We all know if we're miserable at work, it affects our home life. And if we're struggling in our personal life, it impacts our work. These two things have always been intertwined, and with advancements in technology, any separation that existed before has now completely disappeared.

The term that we use shouldn't refer to trading off the two big things in our lives; it should help ensure that they flow better together. That's what Lifeflow is meant to help clarify.

According to a survey of over 20,000 workers by Deloitte in 2022, the three greatest overall sources of stress for people are (1) their long-term financial future, (2) their day-to-day finances, and (3) the welfare of their family.[13] Clearly all of these things are related to both your work and personal life. These two things aren't separated, they're integrated.

The concept of Lifeflow is that your work and home lives

aren't just balanced, they're harmonious. The Workflow model, where life and work are separate, has been in place for over one hundred years. So, understandably, the recent shift to a more integrated Lifeflow model has been challenging for all of us to get our heads around. But approaching things through this lens can be a breakthrough from an employer and employee perspective.

Communicating that Lifeflow is a priority at your company sends a clear message to employees that you care. You're saying that their personal and professional health, and even their wealth, are core and central to how you operate. Health extends beyond physical health to include not just mental health, but even the health of their career and their relationships at work. Wealth includes both financial security as well as wealth of experience you can provide as a company to help grow their long-term financial opportunities for the future.

In that light, sharing that you are addressing isolation as an issue related to both personal and professional health is a much more positive and productive frame for why you want to bring people together. It isn't about the company, it's about them personally. This is a point that many have missed.

Work isn't more important than your life; it is an essential part of it. The relationships that you build are central to your life, not just your career. And the better you feel about your job and the better your company performs, the more it enriches and fulfills you personally and professionally. There doesn't need to be an artificial distinction between your work life and your home life. You have one life. You don't have to sacrifice one for the other; they can and should work together.

As someone who truly values hard work yet never missed moments with my family, I don't want what I'm sharing to be misinterpreted. I am not advocating for working either more or less, but for structuring our lives, and therefore our work, in a more pragmatic fashion. We've all learned that productivity isn't about a place. Many jobs can now be done anywhere. But just because we can doesn't mean we should only work remotely and never be around other people. Relationships and the collective experience of being together are essential to our growth and development. That's the problem to solve right now because it's what's missing the most.

With this pivot to Lifeflow, where work and life are integrated, there is also a newfound flexibility. This brings us to the second shift that is in motion: the move from Factory-Mode to Flex-Mode. Understanding and embracing this will allow us to leverage the power of flex.

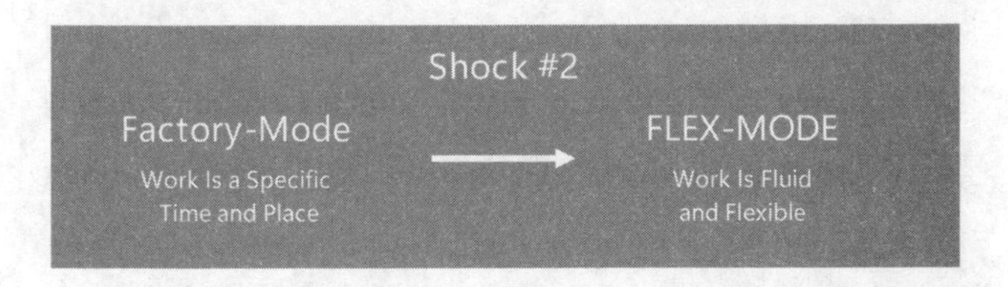

The big shift from *Factory-Mode* to *Flex-Mode* may be the most appealing shock to the system for both employees and employers. When we asked 1,681 CEOs about what makes their company an attractive place to work, the three most common responses were compensation, flexible working hours, and a hybrid or remote working environment. So, two of the top three were about flexibility. And this is not the perspective of folks who work for companies, it's from the folks who run them.

CEOs Chime in on Company Culture

THE QUESTION

What makes your company an attractive place to work?

THE TOP THREE RESPONSES

Compensation
Flexible Work Hours
Hybrid Work Setting

Flex clearly has a great deal of appeal. According to a 2022 survey of 1,500 workers by Topia, flexibility is now the single most compelling quality that people are looking for in a new job.[14] An overwhelming 96 percent rank flexibility as a key factor. A separate survey of 2,500 by Bankrate confirmed the same finding—more people value flexibility than compensation.[15] It feels like every advertisement for a new job now includes flexibility at or near the top of the list. It rivals salary as the number one factor people are looking for in a new job.

We're clearly going through a transition relative to how we structure our work into a more modern model. It took thousands of years for the majority of people to make the move from living and working on a farm to living and working in a factory town. For the last one hundred years, we've been in that same mode of having to be at a physical location to do our work. The pandemic turbocharged a change in that model as we learned many jobs could be done anywhere at any time. In the same way that we shifted from farms to factories over a century ago, we're now moving away from Factory-Mode where work has to be done within the four walls of a building. Instead, we are shifting to Flex-Mode where the majority of work for the majority of people can be done anytime and anywhere. Work is no longer strictly defined by a time or a place.

The power of this change is significant, and fighting against it has proven to be futile. With that said, while flex is appealing, we are also seeing and feeling its limitations. We now need to take a more collaborative approach to ensure that flex is a feature, not a bug.

Make Flex a Feature

The future of how work is structured will include many different approaches. Industries have different considerations, businesses have different needs, roles have different requirements, people have different constraints, and rural, suburban, and urban locations have different commutes. The list goes on and on.

Flex-Mode recognizes these variations are the new norm and new standard. It is very clear that no single solution will work for every industry, company, position, or role. Work location and hours will be based on role and the needs of the company and their employees. Whether and how often people are required to come into an office is going to be very different based on the company, industry, location, etc.

This will play out over time, and for a period of time,

there will continue to be resistance to change. With that said, the one thing that's clear is that some level of flex has a great deal of appeal, not only to the employee, but also to the company.

As an example, this new Flex-Mode has allowed companies to reduce their level of capital invested in their physical space. According to a report in 2022 from Korn Ferry, there will be over 200 million square feet of lease expirations annually through 2025.[16] That is a record level, and with most offices utilizing less than half of their available capacity, there is certainly cause for concern if you're in commercial real estate. Companies are now able to hire people anywhere, creating more velocity in scaling up by adding more people more quickly and opening up their recruitment of employees to a bigger and more diverse talent pool. What's more, many companies have cut down significantly on overall travel expenses while leveraging virtual to be in front of more customers more often.

While there are benefits to each of these, there are also issues. The key is finding the right balance. As an example, clearly there is a difference between someone who just graduated from college who is in their first job and lives ten minutes away; an employee with two kids in grade school who just bought their first house in the suburbs two hours away; and an empty nester who lives in another state. That may sound obvious or extreme, but that's exactly the real-world scenario that I was faced with when trying to determine our go-forward policy. Couple that with the fact that we had just acquired a one-hundred-person company with employees scattered across ten states, and you can begin to see the complexity of creating a single policy that applies to so many unique situations.

There simply is no single path forward. In many ways, the future is already here. We are seeing very different solutions for different companies based on size, industry, and region as well as for different people based on role and position. The Flex Report of 4,000 companies that collectively employ over 100 million people highlights the differences.[17]

Different Strokes for Different Folks

WHERE COMPANIES ARE HYBRID AND WORK REMOTELY THE MOST		WHERE COMPANIES WORK ON-SITE THE MOST	
LOCATIONS	INDUSTRIES	LOCATIONS	INDUSTRIES
Portland	Technology	Memphis	Restaurants
Boulder	Professional Services	New Orleans	Retail and Apparel
Austin	Media & Entertainment	Riverside	Hospitality
Seattle	Financial Services	San Antonio	Manufacturing
Denver	Insurance	Oklahoma City	Healthcare

The industries that are embracing flexibility the most are technology, professional services, media and entertainment, financial services, and insurance. The industries with the most workers on site are restaurants and food services, retail and apparel, hospitality, manufacturing, and healthcare. The metropolitan areas leveraging flexibility the most are Portland, Boulder, Austin, Seattle, and Denver. The metros with the most companies fully on site are Memphis, New Orleans, Riverside, San Antonio, and Oklahoma City. And one last interesting data point is that smaller companies with fewer than five hundred employees are significantly more likely (76 percent) to have taken a flexible approach than companies with over five hundred employees (52 percent).

Embracing this reality helps overcome the myopia of the belief that a single model will emerge. It won't. The answer isn't a single policy—it's a comprehensive strategy. The ultimate issue won't be how many days someone is in an office; it will be understanding what's missing by not having people together and taking action to address it.

In that light, what's missing is clearly a sense of connection. But we need to think very differently about how to create and support it moving forward. Which brings us to the third shock to the system—the movement away from company culture being a collective concept to becoming more of an individual experience.

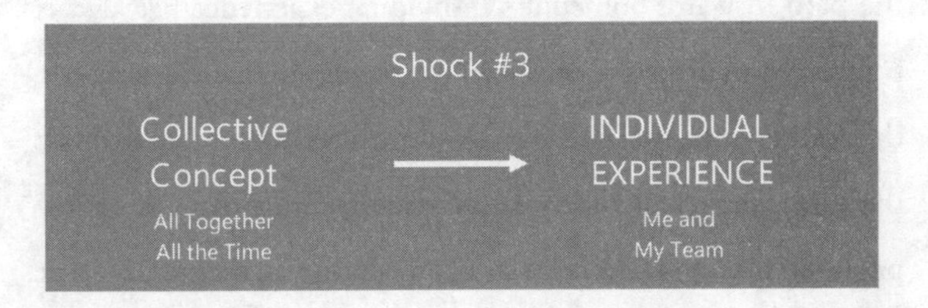

For most people, most of their work experience has been primarily centered around going to a location and being together with others all day every day. Whether in factories, warehouses, office parks, or high-rise towers, this proximity made it relatively easy to connect with others. The human resources team would create ideas, deliver events, and, of course, design office space to help foster this collective experience.

That prior version of what it means to "go to work" is where companies are now struggling the most. Work is no longer just a collective concept; it has become more of an individual experience. This isn't actually a new problem. For decades there has been a trend toward people in a company being more spread out and less connected. Even well-executed company-wide efforts to bring people together have often fallen short of their intent to truly connect with people personally.

If we shift our focus to that reality, we can start to find the path forward. Someone's individual experience has always been what matters the most, which is why the primary metric that most companies use is employee engagement. Many think that the recent challenges we're having in engagement are a new phenomenon and a reflection of generational differences, but the data tells a very different story. What we're experiencing now is nothing new. Companies have had the same employee engagement issues for decades.

Quiet Quitting Is Nothing New

One of the terms that created quite a buzz was "quiet quitting," the idea of essentially doing your job but nothing more, checking off only enough tasks to stay on the payroll. Taking a step back from the emotional reaction at the time, one can see that this was a misread of both the data as well as the moment. The headline "Quiet Quitters Make Up Half the U.S. Workforce" in the *Wall Street Journal* got everyone's attention. It came from a Gallup survey of over fifteen thousand workers based in the US.[18] In their research, Gallup found that one of every five workers was actively disengaged, a concerning number for sure.[19] With that said, that statistic is identical to what it was ten years ago and twenty years ago. In other words, when you dig into the data, it's clear that the only thing that's new about quiet quitting was the name given to it.

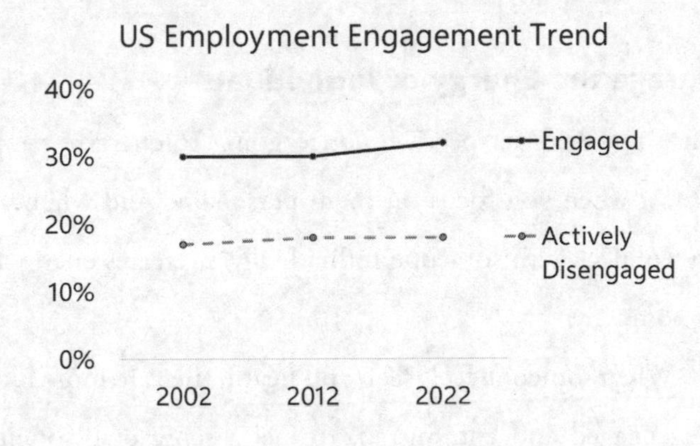

In any case, the term "quiet quitting" turned into a trap that labeled employees as lazy or not wanting to work. It set leaders up to make the mistake of blaming a lack of engagement on the people who work for them. Companies then tried to address engagement issues centrally and collectively at the leadership level. These efforts were, once again, well intentioned but misplaced. To truly drive engagement effectively, the focus needs to be on each person individually and driven by their manager, as they are the ones who can affect it the most. We have to educate, equip, and empower every manager to take the lead to shift our focus to the personal experience of every team member. If you want to create a healthy culture as a company, you need to focus on every person individually.

Leverage the Energy of Individuals

From a practical perspective, you're going to energize people the most when you focus on them personally. And when you really connect with someone individually, it creates energy for your company.

When someone feels seen and heard, they are more likely to be engaged and committed, to feel a sense of belonging, and to build relationships with others. When you better understand someone's specific strengths and weaknesses as well as career aspirations, you can better leverage their talents, build skills, and enhance their contributions to the company. And when you invest time and energy in helping someone grow, you build more trust and increase the likelihood that they will stay with your company for the long term.

Clearly one of the biggest factors in how someone views

their job is the experiences they have with other people in your company. While the number of coworkers someone interacts with on a daily basis is relatively limited for most people, those relationships are absolutely critical. They can be both a source of energy as well as anxiety. In that light, helping to nurture positive and productive relationships within and across teams is mission critical for every company.

The programs that are set up at a corporate or company level are an important element of someone's experience, but they have their limits. And bringing everyone together and implementing initiatives across the company will continue to be key parts of the mix, but they will only take you so far. With the flow of people's lives now more fluid and more flexible work options in place at many companies, extending your focus from what you're doing as a company collectively to the experience of every person individually is more critical than ever before.

Taken together, it's absolutely essential for leaders to recognize and leverage the power of these shocks to the system. The best companies to work for in the future will be the ones who leverage the force of their employees' flow, the power of flex, and the energy of people individually to move their company forward:

- **The Force of Flow:** The best employers will be the ones who fit into the flow of their employees' lives. You don't have a work life and a home life; you have one life, and work can and should be an important part of enhancing it. Things have shifted from Workflow to Lifeflow.
- **The Power of Flex:** Work will be structured differently for every industry, company, position, region, role, and, in many cases, every person. The key for leaders will be to make flex a feature that powers their company forward. We have pivoted from Factory-Mode to Flex-Mode.
- **The Energy of Individuals:** In order to generate the most energy for your company, leaders will need to focus on people personally. There has been a move from working at a company being a Collective Concept to becoming an Individual Experience.

The good news is that these shocks to the system aren't an insurmountable problem; they're an unprecedented opportunity. They can and should inform and impact how we think about what comes next.

Seeing the shifts that we outlined in *STEP ONE: See the Shift* is central to understanding how we got here, but now we have to figure out where to go from here. We are at a major inflection point between the past and the future of work. A seismic shift has happened, and there are forces of nature at play. This is a complex and confusing time, but with something this challenging, the antidote always has to start with attitude. The next step forward in *Holy Shift* is focused on the mindset shifts that can help move your company forward. This is the opportunity of a lifetime for leaders to lead, but only if you can shift your thinking.

STEP TWO
Shift your Mindset

"Culture eats strategy for breakfast."

Peter Drucker
Considered the Founder of the Principles of Modern Management

One of the most oft-repeated quotes on running a high performing company was attributed to the well-respected CEO whisperer and management consultant Peter Drucker. The wisdom of his words is that you can have a world-class strategy, but you'll fall short on execution if you don't have a world-class culture. Say the line "culture eats strategy for breakfast" to any leader or board member, and they'll tell you that they absolutely agree. It's at the top of any list of universal truths of what it takes to run a successful company.

Well, over the last few years, culture didn't just eat strategy for breakfast, it ate it for lunch and dinner as well. As our research reflected and we're all seeing, CEOs are struggling, and there is a crisis of confidence when it comes to company culture. The twists and turns in workplace and workforce dynamics have been hard to process, as we've all seen just how fast and far the pendulum can swing.

In early 2022, with job opportunities and big raises just one mouse click away, power swung to one extreme where an employee felt that their employer was lucky to have them. One year later, it swung to the other extreme as there were major layoffs and employers felt every employee was lucky to have a job.

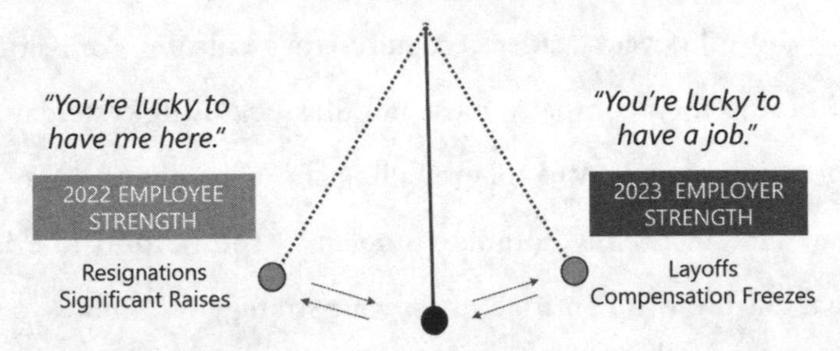

The most important lesson we've learned over time is that any extreme, along with the actions that accompany it, is only temporary. The pendulum will continue to swing and bring us back to somewhere in the middle. With that said, it is clear that going to those extremes took a toll on one thing more than anything—trust.

The existential question for every leader now is how to rebuild that trust. The key will be to make culture central to their overall strategy.

Culture Is the Strategy

Turning culture into the strategy for your company is the first and most important major mindset shift that we'll cover in this section of *Holy Shift*. And mindset really matters if you want to move your company forward to the future of work.

While every leader recognizes that culture is mission critical to their company, most are still stuck using yesterday's tools and tactics. And they're falling short in solving today's new and incredibly complex problems. The bottom line is that culture will continue to eat your strategy . . . unless you turn it into one.

Turning Culture into Strategy

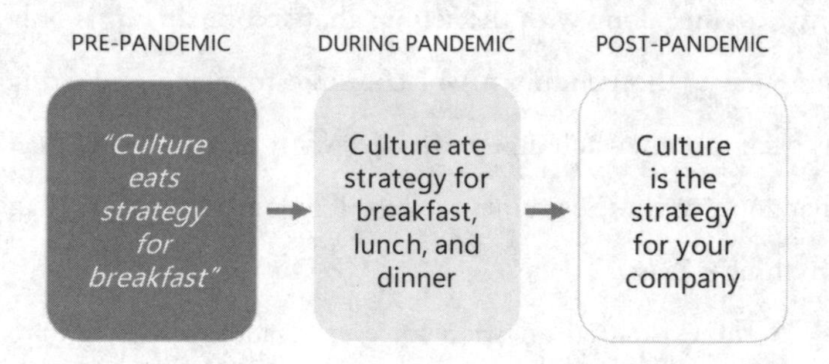

As Drucker also once said, "The greatest danger in times of turbulence is not the turbulence—it is to act with yesterday's logic." When there is a change in the markets that they compete in, leaders are inspired and required to pivot their plans. They need to adopt this same mindset and embrace these shifts in the workplace to help create something new and better for their employees.

The future of work isn't a policy; it's a strategy. It's not about defining a destination with metrics of precision; it's about heading in the right direction where the measure is progression. And the direction that the best companies are heading in isn't *backwards to the past*; they're pressing *forward into the future.* They are leveraging the forces at play; recognizing that your work life and home life now flow together, ensuring that flex is a feature that helps both the company and the employee, and understanding that every single person's journey at your company is an individual experience.

When it comes to change, people often say you have three choices: fight it, ignore it, or embrace it. Mindset is truly a choice and an incredibly important one because, if we shift our thinking to embrace this moment as an opportunity to create momentum, our actions will follow. In that spirit, in *STEP TWO: Shift Your Mindset*, we will cover the five shifts in mindset that can move your company forward:

1. **Shift from Culture as a Tactic to a Strategy:** Companies are no longer looking at culture as a set of *tactics;* they are

putting it at the center of the stage in their *strategy*. The best companies have shifted from human resources owning culture, with leaders as participants, to their leadership team owning culture, with HR as a partner.

2. **Pivot from Bring Back to Bring Together:** The approach to bring people *back* and the way it was communicated created a chasm of conflict between leaders and their teams. Leaders now need to shift to a more positive and collaborative long-term strategy that can help bring people *together*.

3. **Migrate from Macro to Micro:** Companies have always approached culture with the expectation that everything an employee will experience at your company can be created and implemented centrally. That time has passed, and there is now a migration from *macro* to *micro,* a movement to focus on improving what people actually experience directly on a daily basis.

4. **Move from Managing to Coaching:** The track record of *managing* with an authority-figure type of approach isn't great, and it's becoming increasingly ineffective. The best leaders have moved to a *coaching*-based approach that is

more positive and collaborative, where a coach views the people on their team as working with them, not for them.

5. **Evolve from Evaluation to Conversation:** The traditional approach of how people are evaluated is hard coded into everything we do. Evaluations have a place, but their use is often misguided in the workplace. Companies are evolving from *evaluations* that often lead to confrontation, to *conversations* that drive collaboration.

The first and most important shift in mindset is how you and your team look at the importance of company culture to begin with. Given how much leaders feel is now at risk and on the line when it comes to their team, it's time to get more strategic.

CHAPTER FIVE

Shift to Culture as the Strategy

MINDSET SHIFT #1

Culture is a Tactic	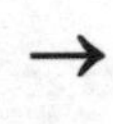	CULTURE IS THE STRATEGY

THE KEY TO CREATING a world-class culture in any company is evolving beyond short-term tactics to a more long-term, sustainable strategy that truly benefits both your company and everyone on your team. Yes, this can be done, but it will require a number of significant changes.

The first change is that many companies are moving away from their human resources team owning culture, with their leadership team as participants, to their leadership team owning culture, with HR as a partner in the process. This is a major shift from the standard in most companies, where the human resources team was responsible for creating and implementing everything. In the past, this included everything from company events and celebrations to community initiatives. This approach worked pretty well at times in a centralized model where everyone was in the same place at the same time. But now that companies are more spread out and our experience at work is more distributed, we need to think differently. Every leader has to get on board, and every manager will ultimately have to own the employee experience for each member of their team.

The second change is that leaders are evolving beyond short-term tactics and shifting their focus to creating an overall long-term strategic plan for their company culture. As I have spent time with many CEOs and leaders on this topic, I've proposed one simple goal—for everyone on your team, you want to make this job the best job they have ever had and the best place they have ever worked. Having that or something similar as a goal creates a broader strategic frame for elevating the experience for members of your team. After all, strategy isn't about precision, it's about direction, and that's what everyone on every team is looking for from their leaders right now.

Strategy Is a Direction, Not a Destination

The word *strategy* means many different things to different people, so let me take a shot at simplifying. I've spent over twenty years deep in strategic-planning roles, in the trenches as an analyst, as an advisor to hundreds of companies, as the Chief Strategy Officer for a public company, and as the CEO of the company that I led for the last decade. I also teach a course on decision strategy at a graduate school. I say all of that just so I can share one key lesson—strategy is about a direction, not a destination.

Leaders often fall flat in their planning as they try to be too specific. There are always going to be many uncertainties. Think of it this way. When people approach strategy as a destination, they view it as if they're going on a trip to Miami, will catch a plane at 10:20 in the morning, grab a ride-share, and arrive at their hotel at 4:00 in the afternoon. And they have a set itinerary for every activity and every meal.

This is how many leaders approached the last few years. They made proclamations and spoke with certainty in a time of chaos, only to have to reverse course over and over again. They then tried to go back to their old tactical plan, only to realize what worked in the past was now falling flat. I made the same mistakes. My old playbook also included leveraging an attractive office space and an endless stream of benefits among many other things, but those tactics simply aren't resonating with anyone anymore.

The mistake many are making is proclaiming that the future of work is a precise destination when they should be sharing more of a general direction. The endless stream of starts and stops has exhausted people and created significant animosity. Given that most CEOs and leaders missed the mark on their back-to-the-office policy, now is the right time to reflect, rethink, and reenergize about where you're heading from here.

When it comes to setting your direction, the right frame is more like a road trip. The most important decision is that you're going to head south. Your plan may be to go to Miami, but you're going to make some stops along the way. You might end up in Nashville and stay there or decide to leave and head to Memphis. You may never end up in Miami, and that's just fine.

That's how every strategy actually plays out over time in any company. While it's nice to hope that someday you'll get to a specific destination, it's critical to be clear to folks on your trip that Miami isn't your surefire destination and that the road ahead will likely involve twists and turns along the way.

Shift to Culture as the Strategy

Welcome to the future of work.

The best leaders have set a new direction to make company culture the mission-critical strategy for their company. And they're making major investments to back it up. Analysts estimate that over $300 billion is now spent annually by companies on employee experience.[20] Unfortunately, that alone isn't enough. The new twist and turn in the road is that putting more money into what we've done in the past simply won't work anymore. Things have changed; shift has happened. Culture can no longer be just a list of tactics. It now needs to be a big part of the strategy for your company. It's time to throw away the old roadmap and set out on a new road trip together.

Shifting Your Mindset to Culture Is the Strategy

Here are five steps you can take to *shift* from treating culture as a tactic to turning it into the strategy for your company:

1. **Ensure the Leadership Team Owns Culture:** Shift from HR owning culture, with leaders as participants, to leadership owning culture, with HR as a partner. This is exactly what your HR team wants and needs. The mistake many leaders have made in the past is delegating the creation of

their culture to their human resources team. Recognizing that we are going through an incredibly complex time, it is now the right time to challenge and move away from that way of thinking.

2. **Set Stretch Targets with a Proactive Push:** It's important to set an inspiring target that resonates with your team and drives daily actions on the ground. While it's helpful to have metrics like employee net promoter score and employee retention as trailing indicators for the leadership team, they don't translate to or inspire employees. They also put the leadership team in react mode, where they are worrying about their score. A more proactive push and stretch target is to set a target of trying to make this the single best job experience for every person on the team. This will place the focus on constantly trying to level it up for each person individually. This shift from being reactive as a company to being proactive with people individually is an important step in the right direction.

3. **Create a Strategic Framework:** Now that you have a proactive and ambitious target, you will need to have a plan. In order for your plan to be easy to understand

and execute, it is helpful to have a strategic framework. In *STEP THREE: Make Shift Happen*, we outline an approach called CORE, which focuses on the four factors that have the highest correlation to employee productivity, engagement, and retention. Also, with any strategy, your plan will require a defined level of investment. One of the mistakes many companies are making is baking the savings from less travel and fewer people in the office into their baseline plan. Specific investments, like allocating dollars for bringing teams together, have to be seen as strategic—a need-to-have, not just a nice-to-have. As any executive would admit, if you want to understand if someone has a strategy, all you need to do is look at their budget.

4. **Clearly Communicate with Candor:** When it comes to most companies, miscommunication and a lack of clear, consistent communication from leadership is the norm. While as a leader you may think everyone is on the same page, you're better off assuming that no one understands what you're talking about. This has always been a challenge, but employees in both on-site and remote companies are now more spread out, which has made matters worse. The

most important thing that leaders can do moving forward is to own and manage the message. At times, uncertainty has been the enemy that has stood in the way of communicating with clarity, but this can be addressed by openly acknowledging the unknowns. The key to overcoming any mistakes in the past or in the future is to speak with candor. Moving forward, it's critical to have a solid communication plan for sharing your strategy. To that end, the first step is acknowledging what people have gone through and how things have changed. The second is articulating and owning the problems of the past and articulating any ongoing issues and challenges. The third is sharing the strategy that is being set in motion and how they will need to help in order to make it work. The final step is maintaining a cadence of communication over time, keeping the team in the loop as you make progress toward your plan and encounter new challenges in the future. As we have detailed, we are in the middle of a monumental change in how we work. But the anxiety around this can be managed as long as you clearly communicate that things can and will change and assure the team that you will work through these things together.

5. **Adapt and Adjust:** With any strategy, or any road trip for that matter, the journey is the destination. While the path ahead is not completely clear, as long as everyone understands this, they can get on board and enjoy the ride. To that end, it's critical to be agile and adjust your plan over time. Leveraging an approach where your plan is reviewed at a regular cadence is key, as things will continue to change. We're all learning as we go. If we embrace that uncertainty and communicate about it honestly and openly with our teams, we will all end up in a better place.

Having your leadership own, create, and clearly communicate that culture is a core strategy for your company is a good start. But the details of the plan are what's most important.

To that end, the center of any strategy needs to address the primary problem, which is the lack of connection between members of the team. Up until now, we have distilled that into a pretty combative tactic of bringing people *back*. It's time to shift to a more robust and uplifting strategy focused on how to bring people *together*.

CHAPTER SIX

Pivot from Bring Back to Bring Together

MINDSET SHIFT #2

Bring Back	→	BRING TOGETHER
Move Backward		Move Forward

WHEN IT COMES to effectively implementing any strategy, ensuring that it has the right focus and is communicated in the right way really matters.

Unfortunately, this is exactly where leaders missed the mark over the last few years. The tactics that were used and the way they were communicated created a chasm of conflict between leaders and their teams. Trust levels declined, and morale suffered. But all that can change; it's not too late.

There is one quality that all great leaders and managers have in common—they build trust. But a recent Gallup survey revealed a shocking result: only two out of ten employees strongly agree that they can trust the leadership of their organization.[21] Our independent research resulted in the identical outcome.

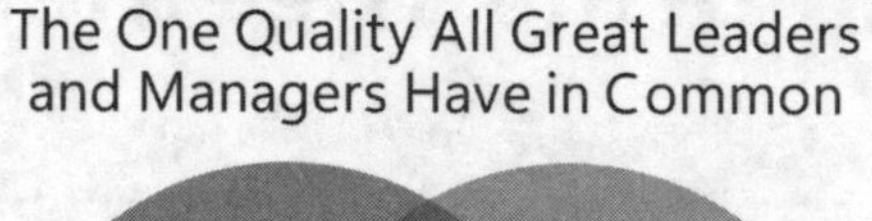

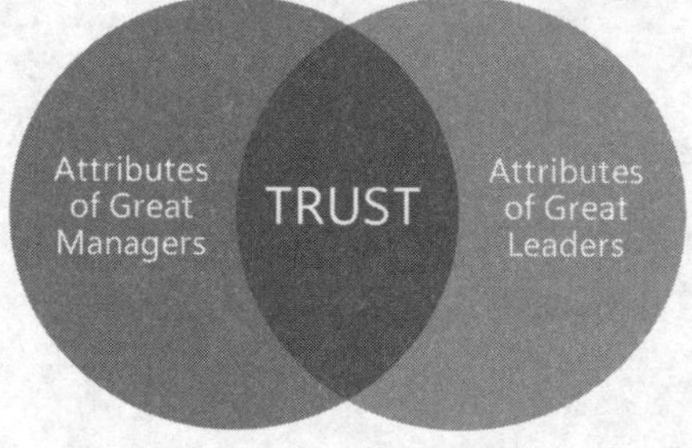

The good news is that nine of ten employees say they fully trust their leaders when they do the following: (1) inspire confidence in the future, (2) lead and support change, and (3) communicate clearly. In that light, one of the key steps that leaders can take to rebuild trust is to shift away from confrontational short-term tactics on how to bring people *back*, and instead embrace a more collaborative long-term strategy that can help bring people *together*. First let's take a step back to understand how we got here so we can determine where to go from here.

"Bring Back" Came Across as an Attack

Communication is central to our ability to rally our teams, but when it's not done right, it can create chaos. The term "bring back to work" became the central rallying cry for CEOs with their companies. The thought process for many was that bringing their people back into the office would bring back their culture. While well-intentioned, it wasn't seen that way by employees.

As our research demonstrated, over time, CEOs came to believe that their team could be productive in any setting, so the intent to bring people back was more about the other benefits they saw that came from being together. But the implication of the term "bring back to work" was that you weren't working at home. This sent a clear signal that there was a lack of trust—and that's not good.

Our survey showed that CEOs' true concern was that they felt being together was critical for collaboration, employee development, and relationship building. These are actually all good things for the company and for everyone's career. But the initial communication left the impression that people were being "forced" to come back. This narrative wasn't helping company culture; it was killing it.

With that said, the bigger problem is that the term didn't communicate a comprehensive strategy to bring the company *forward* to the future. Instead, it sent a clear signal that you were implementing a single tactic to bring the company *back* to where it was in the past. That's not to say that determining the number of days per week that people need to be in the office isn't a critical decision. The issue was that the way it was communicated caused conflict.

The list of problems with this approach and this line of communication goes on and on. For this reason, it's time to drop that narrative and pivot to more positive and strategic positioning. And a great way to do this is to think through a strategy that is focused on the job to be done.

The Job to Be Done

As the renowned and respected Harvard professor and author Clayton Christiansen would often say, the best way to build a product, process, or strategy is to start by understanding the "job to be done." This concept is based on the idea that you essentially hire a company, or buy one of its products, to do a job for you. Understanding this provides remarkable clarity on what your customers truly value, which is often different than what you thought.

In that light, this is a very good model for leaders to use to design the experience they want to deliver for their employees. It flips the thinking. For example, when it comes to working at your company, what are your employees actually *hiring you* as a leader to do and what do they expect from you? In that same spirit, if they leave, why are they *firing you*?

Often people default to *compensation* as the answer to every question and miss the mark completely on the essence of employee engagement, which boils down to *expectations*. Just like when you buy any product or service, if the experience doesn't match expectations you will switch to something else. Or, in this case, you'll quit your job and go work for someone else.

So, stop for a second, apply Christiansen's framework, and think of people coming to work for your company this way. They are paying you with their time and talent as well as their effort and energy. In exchange, your company is providing a few things that have a great deal of value: compensation, opportunities to grow, a connection to others, and a sense of identity and purpose. The problem to be solved is that even if you get compensation right, most companies are still falling short on three of the four.

One of the places where leaders are really missing the mark the most is in driving a sense of purpose with their team. A study by McKinsey confirmed this in a striking fashion.

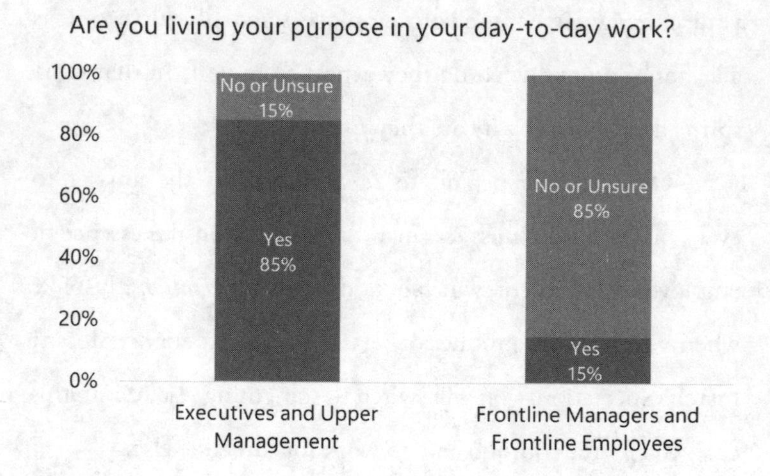

When people were asked if they are living their purpose in their day-to-day work, 85 percent of executives and upper management said they can live their purpose in their daily work versus only 15 percent of frontline managers and employees.[22]

In that light, the "job to be done" for leaders is to address this gap and ensure employees feel a sense of purpose and connection to the company. Leaders instinctively know this, which is why they focused on tactics to bring people back to the office. The issue is that the message should have been framed around how a return to the office helps the employee, not the company. It shouldn't be about the necessity of bringing people back but about the benefits of being together.

In light of that, the job to be done for leaders is to shift from tactics that cause confusion and conflict, to a strategy that is clear, collaborative, compelling, and forward looking for your company. A strategy that sets everyone on the team up to contribute to the company and grow personally over time. But just having the right strategy is never enough; you need to get your team on board. As every leader in every walk of life inevitably learns, your message really matters.

It's about Bringing People Together

In the lead-up to the 1992 presidential election, James Carville famously crystalized what the narrative needed to be for Bill Clinton with the line, "It's the economy, stupid." Ronald Reagan had taken the same approach to rally his team in 1980.

Both won and served for two terms as the president of the United States. They had superpower skills when it came to communication. They understood the essence of the emotion and rooted it in something very rational.

Whether it's a candidate communicating a message to their team or a CEO sharing their strategy with their company, providing that level of clarity and connecting with people in a way that's both personal and emotional is critical. In that spirit, a way-too-blunt way to communicate to your leaders about what they really need to do to bring your company forward is—"It's about bringing people together, stupid."

Of course, I wouldn't suggest using that exact language unless you wanted to direct it at me. I have made many stupid mistakes; this has been a confusing time for all of us. But all leaders now have to help their teams cut through the clutter and focus on the core of the problem that needs to be solved. The job to be done isn't to bring people back; it's to bring them together. And that's a message that has benefits for every single person in your company.

A survey of close to 6,000 workers by the Pew Research Center revealed that the number one issue of working remotely was the lack of connection with others.[23] Inspiring people to feel truly connected to your culture and their coworkers is critical to your company and everyone on your team's career. For these reasons, if you want to turn culture into a strategy, both your message and actions have to be centered on bringing people together.

Shifting Your Mindset from Bring Back to Bring Together

Here are five steps you can take to *shift* the mindset of your company from bringing back to bringing together:

1. **Refocus Your Strategy:** As we outlined in Chapter Five, leaders must own both creating a strategy and taking the lead on how best to bring the company together. While this includes the tactic of how often people on their team need to come in, it needs to evolve and extend beyond that. Even if your team is in an office, most are still isolated from those around them. There is work to do to help people better connect with each other, and we will cover that in more detail in *STEP THREE: Make Shift Happen.* With that said, the starting point of determining how, when, and where to bring people together will drive investments that

you make as a company. Because of this, involving your entire leadership team, including your CFO or finance leader, in this strategy is critical. But any decisions that you make around physical space or employee travel, for example, can't simply be financial decisions. They have to be grounded in a strategy that is supported by the appropriate level of investment.

2. **Create a Comprehensive Plan:** Once your strategy is set, it's time to define the details. This includes determining what is needed for the company overall and for each function, team, and role. This includes any in-person requirements for employees, as well as investments in events, programs, and processes in your plan. Ensuring your plan leverages in-person and virtual settings effectively is critical. Per a paper published in the MIT Sloan Management Review, in-person interactions are essential for energizing relationships, creating a sense of purpose and providing job feedback.[24] Once that foundation is in place, it is critical to get the message right and get the entire company on board.

3. **Make Your Approach Crystal Clear:** Providing clarity on

whether an in-office presence is required for each person relative to their role, level, and function, as well as the rationale behind it is critical. Different roles, levels, and functions have different needs, and it's important to make that clear. A human resources team may need to be in the office, while a sales team has always been, and likely will always be, remote. A project manager is a role that requires constant collaboration, whereas a developer can and will often work independently. Managers, in general, are responsible for the development of their team, so at times, they need to be in the office to mentor others in person. This is a perfectly reasonable expectation that often isn't articulated with that level of clarity.

4. **Invest in Bringing People Together:** Like many leaders, for many years I relied on all-hands meetings where everyone would pile into one room for an update. While it may have been boring to some and redundant to others, it served as a simple and straightforward approach to keeping everyone in sync. Some have kept that cadence going in a virtual setting, but this approach often falls flat. There will need to be new focus and energy applied to where, when, and how to bring teams together in person

as a group. This applies to remote as well as hybrid and on-site companies. This is a huge point because what you did in the past won't get you where you want and need to be in the future. I learned this lesson the hard way, but now it's time to pivot. As stated earlier, it's a mistake to not set aside the required investment to bring your people together. This is penny-wise in the short-term and pound-foolish in the long-term.

5. **Change the Narrative:** As we have outlined, having a great strategy with good intentions is not enough. It is crucial to clearly communicate the purpose in a way that motivates people to move forward. Recognizing that every company will take a somewhat different approach, here's a message you can send to your employees to use as a starting point:

   SUBJECT: Moving Forward into the Future . . . Together

   In reflecting as a leadership team on some of the challenges over the last few years, we think we've found a better way to bring our team forward from here. We believe we have a unique opportunity to deliver the best of both worlds—flexibility from a personal perspective coupled with growth from a professional perspective. We are working on a strategy that is focused on you—your enjoyment of your job and your opportunity to contribute to the company. To make that happen, we believe it is absolutely essential to provide you with experiences and moments to learn directly from others, build relationships, work as part of a team, and feel part of a community. To that end, we're creating an approach where we can bring people together in ways that are both helpful and productive for everyone on the team. We truly care about you and want your experience at work to be an extraordinary one. While we believe it is absolutely mission critical for all of us to come together collectively, we will be flexible in our approach and make every effort to accommodate the constraints of people individually. Our commitment to every member of our team is that we will work with you to find the best ways to ensure that you feel connected to our company and our culture as well as your coworkers. We have a lot to figure out, and things will take shape over time. With that said, I would encourage you to lean in and share your thoughts and ideas. We all have an opportunity to play a part in building a best practice and world-class company. We're truly excited about our future and creating something even better . . . together.

This message only provides a starting point. Once a more defined long-term strategy is in place, you should add in the specific requirements for each role and expectations for the company overall. That clarity is critical.

But even if your leadership team owns, creates, communicates, and executes a strong strategy and plan relative to overall company culture, it won't get you even halfway to where you need to be. Unfortunately, there are limits to the ability of any leadership team to impact the actual on-the-ground, day-to-day experience for people in the company. In order to really get traction, we need to make another mindset shift, from macro to micro.

CHAPTER SEVEN

Migrate from Macro to Micro

MINDSET SHIFT #3

Macro	→	MICRO
Our Company		Me and My Circle

WHEN IT COMES to creating a strategic plan for anything, it has to be focused and targeted. In that light, to create a fresh and forward-thinking plan for your company relative to culture, there are two levels that you'll need to nail. The first level is what you do across the company; let's refer to that as your *macro* or broader strategy. The second level is what you do within teams and for each person directly, let's refer to as your *micro* or targeted strategy.

In a macro approach, the definition of culture is feeling connected to the company vision, mission, and values. In that light, it's critical what the company says and shares. By this definition, for almost everyone in your company, culture is something that they only experience occasionally.

Companies have always approached culture as more of a macro concept, where everything that an employee will experience at your company is created and implemented centrally. But with the massive changes in how and where we work, we now need to think very differently. The primary focus of our strategy has to shift from macro to micro . . . meaning me and my circle.

The Need to Evolve from Macro to Micro

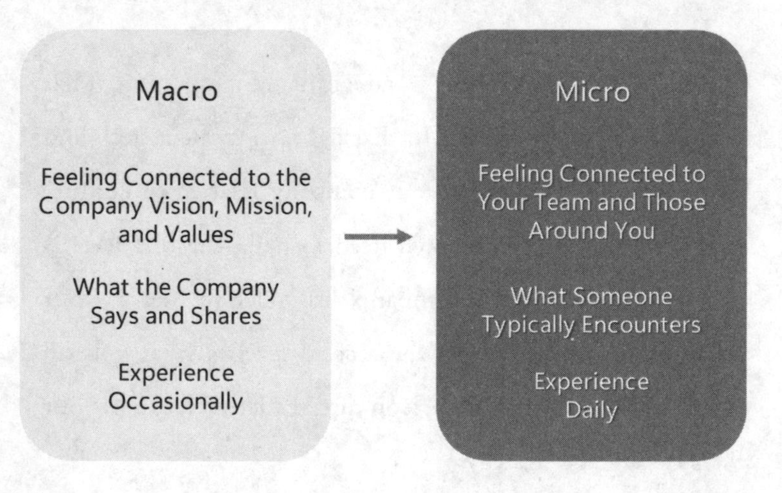

Think of micro in a very simple way: what matters most is what people experience directly on a daily basis. In all walks of life, we spend the majority of our time with a relatively small number of people. That's also true for most people within a company. Most of us, including leaders, only interact with just a few people on our team or across teams every day. That small (micro) circle is what affects our overall (macro) experience at a company more than anything.

Relative to your company, picture everyone on your team having a circle around them. For some, that circle is small, and for others, it's pretty big. For some, those connections and relationships are strong, for others, perhaps, pretty weak. Either way, that circle is their reality and what defines their experience at your company. And for most people, the center of that circle is their manager. That's the relationship that matters the most.

My Manager Matters the Most

Imagine that you are a principal at a grade school. You set a wonderful example as a leader and provide all of the right resources for your teachers. You are well respected, and your school is recognized as one of the best in the state. You're at the top of your game and the peak of your powers. One day a parent asks for a meeting with you and shares that their child is struggling in one of their classes. Your first thought is, "Let's talk with their teacher." That is the moment when every principal both recognizes and acknowledges the fact that their ability to affect every student in their school has its limits. Clearly, the only thing that matters to that parent is their child's experience in that classroom with that teacher.

In that same vein, CEOs and leaders have limits in their ability to affect the experience of every person in their company. Just like teachers with students, managers are going to have the biggest impact on employees.

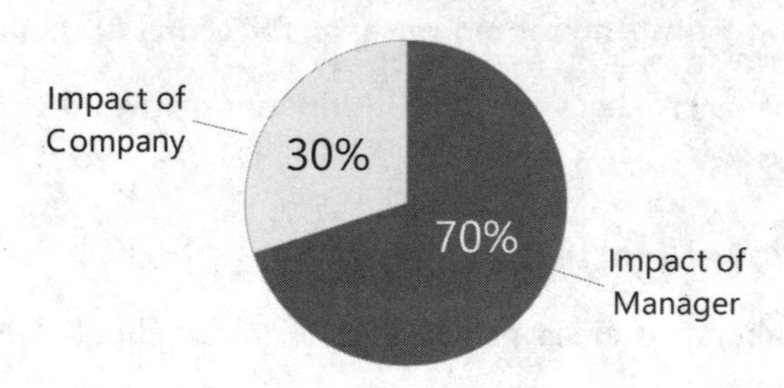

According to research by Gallup, 70 percent of an employee's engagement at work is driven by the one-to-one relationship with their manager.[25] Stop and think about that for a moment. When it comes to someone's experience at your company, that stunning stat should stop leaders in their tracks. It means that the majority of someone's experience at your company is out of your direct control; it's in the hands of your managers.

Many of us have had a mindset that an employee's relationship was ultimately with the company. In my own experience, there was no limit to the things that I would do to reach and impact every person. I would pour my heart and soul into every message and every all-hands meeting. I had an endless number of coaching and mentoring meetings and sent personal messages to everyone, constantly. Over the course of a decade as CEO, I spent over half of my time focused on our team, only to now find out that managers mattered much more than I did. To be clear, it wasn't that I didn't understand this on a practical level. But the reality was that all of our time, effort, energy, and investment had been at the macro or company level, when at least 70 percent of it should have been focused on the micro or team level.

Stepping away from the data and reflecting on our own experiences, I don't think the importance of our relationship with our manager would surprise any of us. In the same way that a teacher can create or crater the experience of a class, our relationship with our manager can have an enormous positive or negative impact on both our professional and personal life. When you have a bad relationship with your manager, it's a dark cloud hanging over your head that won't go away. It causes an enormous amount of stress that you can feel at night and on weekends—it's always there. On the other hand, when you have a good relationship, it shines a light and inspires you to contribute and grow in ways that you didn't know you could.

With that said, it is important to recognize that everyone's experience is an individual one. Just as there can be two students in the same class with the same teacher where one is struggling and the other is thriving, the same is true on every team with every manager in your company. Understanding that is critical, because work is ultimately an individual experience.

It's More About "Me" Than "We"

You can live in a great city, but absolutely hate it. You can go to a great school, but have a horrible experience. And you can work for a great company, but feel it's the worst job that you've ever had. It doesn't mean that the city, school, or company isn't doing the right things; it just isn't working in the right way for *you*.

Migrate from Macro to Micro

When we approach culture in a macro framework, we are thinking of things in terms of *we*, the things we are doing collectively for the team as a whole. But none of that matters if the experience isn't a good one for *me*. In other words, it's more about *me* than *we*.

One of the struggles that we are starting to better understand is how people are often not "seen" in a company. Going back to the school example, imagine you are a parent sitting down with that teacher to discuss your child, the challenges they are having, and the stress it is causing. The teacher responds that the rest of the class is thriving, but let's talk it through and see what we can do. The obvious implication is that your child is the one with the problem, and we need to find a way to fix them. How does that make you feel? Does the fact that the rest of the class is doing well matter to you? Of course not, what matters is your child and getting them to a better place.

In the context of the workplace, we often make this same mistake. The job to be done is to understand how everyone feels about their experience and empower managers to improve it. What we used to manage centrally now needs to be implemented in a more distributed fashion. If managers are the ones who ultimately drive someone's enjoyment of their job, we have to make sure we are giving them the tools and the training to do it right.

Moving forward, if we want to do big things for our company, we need to think small. We have to recognize the reality that there are limits to what human resources and the leadership team can control centrally. Returning to the academic example, our focus and our resources need to shift from the school as a whole to each individual classroom and teacher so we can help improve the experience of every single student. Every student truly matters—and the same is true for every person in your company. Macro is an important concept, but micro is what ultimately matters.

In any company, that micro experience for an employee is directly related to the people they connect, communicate, and interact with on a daily basis. The ability to understand that circle for each employee and help them build meaningful and trusting relationships is where we need to focus moving forward.

Shifting Your Mindset from Macro to Micro

Here are five steps you can take to *shift* the mindset of your company from macro to micro:

Migrate from Macro to Micro

1. **Resource and Empower Teams:** Communicate to your managers that the experience of each member on their team is a top priority and that they have to own it. While this helps empower them, you'll also want to make sure to resource it effectively. This may require reallocating resources from other budgets or investing incrementally. Some companies allocate a team fund that can be used for social outings as well as for education and other development activities. With that said, not everything requires money. One example is setting aside one day per year to have a team day where they can decide how they spend the time and what they want to do with it. While this loss of control may feel a little disorientating to some, the level of autonomy and trust that it communicates is empowering. Still, it is fine and, in many cases, helpful to provide some level of direction, such as making it a priority to focus on community service while giving managers and teams the autonomy to choose how, where, and when they serve. The experience will help bring the team closer together and likely have a bigger impact than anything you could have done centrally and collectively as a company.

2. **Methodically Mentor Managers:** For most companies, the development of managers is a bit of a free-for-all. While there are exceptions, most managers don't receive the right level of guidance or access to the right types of resources and tools that can help them accelerate their growth and development. They may have some form of training, but it is typically basic, and access is sporadic at best. They may take in-person classes or engage in online learning, but very little of what they learn is situational and contextual. With that said, the biggest issue is that they aren't trained on or being given tools for what matters the most—relationship building. Moving this aspect of management from strictly art and experience based to science and tool based must be a focus if employee experience is a priority for your company.

3. **Focus on Strengthening Someone's Circle:** As we have outlined, the people that someone interacts with, both inside and outside their team, have an enormous impact on their enjoyment of their job. It follows that one of the best ways you can improve their experience is by strengthening that circle. The first step is to understand what that circle looks like for everyone individually, which is a great

conversation for a manager to have with a member of their team. The next step is to identify the strength and impact of those relationships. Are they strong or weak relationships? Positive or negative? This is an incredibly important set of questions. As an example, let's say a director of one team has a horrible relationship with the leader of another team, causing a tremendous amount of friction across the company. Clearly that's a negative relationship that is affecting those two people and many others where you need to lean in to help, even though most leaders don't. In many ways, that's an easy situation and scenario; you can see it and feel it. For other members of the team, what's more challenging is uncovering issues that you *can't* see—that can only be uncovered through conversation. While some situations can be challenging, the action that all managers must take is to help members of their team build relationships and get better connected with others in the company.

4. **Focus on Level of Impact:** The key to any macro or company-wide effort is the level of impact on an individual level. But the primary measure of a single employee benefit you offer or event you host isn't employee retention rates or engagement scores. It's too difficult to tie

anything back directly. The more critical metric when it comes to anything you set in motion centrally is a micro measure—*participation rate*. I learned this the hard way. A few years back, we created an extra education stipend, $500 of "seed money" to invest in every employee. Each person had the autonomy to use it however they wanted, as long as they could tie it back in some way to the company. And after they were done, they gave a ten-minute presentation to share what they had learned to inspire others. I was super proud of the program . . . and super disappointed to find out that a few years later less than 20 percent of the company was participating. It was a tough pill to swallow, but this was the measure that mattered. It wasn't hitting the mark, so we dropped the program. This is one of many examples where, despite good intentions, there wasn't a great result. Another example was our volunteer programs. This one provides a sad but hopeful truth. When we had our human resources team plan community events, the same twenty people would show up every time. A sad showing for a five-hundred-person company. But when we stopped that central approach and instead delegated the opportunity to create community activities down to individual teams, every person on even a twenty-person team would show up. Not a surprise, right? That's exactly the way we need to think moving forward. If it's at the company level, it's all about participation rate, otherwise shift to the team level. It works better, and it's no surprise that that's not a surprise to anyone.

5. **Understand and Improve Individual Experience:** Employee engagement surveys are a good tool for benchmarking and evaluating overall macro-level themes across a company. With that said, they don't measure the most important thing, which is understanding someone's individual feelings about their experience at your company. It is critical that we find other ways that extend beyond employee engagement surveys to open up a direct dialogue between managers and their team members about their own individual experience. To that end, a manager needs be able to build trust within their team. The most important thing leadership can do to instill that skill is to invest in the training and tools to support them.

Whenever we create a plan, make investments, or build programs or processes, we have to think in terms of the level of impact. In the case of culture, the metrics that matter are the number of people we're reaching and how the initiative or program is affecting their experience in the company.

Perhaps surprisingly, it turns out that leaders actually have very little leverage. Leaders' ability to affect someone's individual experience is limited; we need to rely on our managers and help them make the mental shift from being a manager to becoming a coach.

CHAPTER EIGHT
Move from Managing to Coaching

MINDSET SHIFT #4

Managing		COACHING
You Work for Me		We Work Together

Making the shift from a manager mindset to that of a coach creates one thing more than anything—trust. This comes from taking a personal interest in people and showing that you truly care. A company can shower people with endless benefits, but all of it is useless if someone doesn't feel a sense of connection with their manager.

A study by the Workforce Institute revealed that managers

have the same level of impact on someone's mental health as their significant other, and an even bigger impact than their doctor or therapist.[26] And less than one in five people feel that their performance is managed in a way that motivates them to do outstanding work.[27]

Making progress in building trust and a close connection in the work setting requires an ongoing conversation, not just an occasional evaluation. And that won't happen unless the manager understands that their job really isn't to manage, it's to be a coach.

A Single Goal for Every Manager

To understand the power of this pivot, let's make it personal. Think of the best teacher or coach you've ever had. Now think of why they hit that mark. It's likely that they took a personal interest in you. You felt seen by them; they made you feel special. They recognized something inside of you and tried to help you build on it. On the flip side, think of the worst teacher or coach you ever had. There is a good chance they did the exact opposite. If every manager could understand that frame of reference, it would change the game.

But managers are clearly struggling with the stress of

falling short. Per that same study by the Workforce Institute referenced earlier, managers early in their career have the highest level of unhappiness at work of any role in the company.

Managers Aren't Having Fun Yet

1 of 2
Said they will likely quit their job due to stress at work

1 of 2
Wished someone had warned them not to take their job

Over half of managers wished someone had warned them not to take their job. The majority also said they will likely quit their job in the next year due to work-related stress. Reframing the role from a manager to a coach is part of the recipe to help address this and reimagine this responsibility.

My mom taught school in the inner city for thirty-three years and saved every note that she ever received from her students. How great is that? In that spirit, every leader and manager should set one simple goal, and it's not to be a great *manager*. Instead, they should set a goal to try to be the best *coach* that someone has ever had. They will know that they hit the mark if they get a note like the ones my mom received. After all, impacting someone else's life is the only grade that really matters. That's why we have to stop managing and start coaching.

Be a Coach

The track record of managing, teaching, or even coaching with an authority figure type of approach isn't great, and it's becoming increasingly ineffective and problematic. The power imbalance creates a distance between a manager and those who work for them.

In contrast, a coaching-based approach to managing is positive and collaborative, where a coach views the people on their team as working *with* them, not *for* them. Managers must become more like coaches in order to effectively lead and motivate their teams. Today's workforce is more diverse and dynamic than ever and less inclined to respond positively to top-down decision-making and strict hierarchies. They are looking for leaders who can connect with them on a personal level, provide guidance and support, and empower them.

Coaching is a more flexible and adaptable management style. A coach listens actively, provides constructive feedback, and helps their team members develop their own solutions to problems. This type of approach fosters trust, collaboration, and continuous learning, which are all essential for driving innovation and growth. They help their team members navigate through difficult times and adapt to new challenges, developing resilience and adaptability. This helps managers keep their teams engaged, motivated, and productive. That sounds pretty good, doesn't it? Here's how you can make the shift.

Shifting Your Mindset from Managing to Coaching

Here are five steps you can take to *shift* the mindset of your company from managing to coaching:

1. **Provide Guidance, Not Direction:** A coach provides personal support and guidance to each individual team member, helping them to identify and overcome their unique challenges and achieve their goals. This is more effective than a manager who may have a one-size-fits-all approach. New managers really struggle with this concept, especially when they have been promoted to managing their peers. They tend to fall into the trap of thinking everyone now needs to follow their personal

playbook and take an approach of leading by example. This is why elite athletes often struggle as coaches as they take a "do what I do" approach. It is critical to help coach managers that they need to provide guidance versus dictate direction.

2. **Focus on Superpower Skills:** Traditional managers tend to take a narrow focus on the *hard* skills required for the specific role that an individual is in right now. In contrast, a coach extends their focus to also help that person build more effective *soft* skills, such as communication and collaboration, which are essential for working together with others and growing their career. They help identify those critical soft skills, coach an individual in real-time situations, reflect on specific examples, and provide tools and training to help them develop skills over time. But calling them "soft" skills implies that they aren't hard to acquire and they lack substance. Nothing could be further from the truth. They come up in every performance review. A slight shift to calling them *superpower* skills more accurately reflects how these skills can help you professionally. Hard skills are the foundational skills required to do your job. But it's your superpower skills, formerly known as soft

skills, that give you the ability to significantly level up in your job and over your career.

3. **Encourage Self-Awareness and Personal Growth:** A coach helps team members understand their strengths and weaknesses and what they need to do in order to improve and grow. They identify the appropriate training and development opportunities to help someone reach their full potential, which also translates into building a more skilled and capable team over time. Managers tend to focus on their own needs over the needs of an individual. Moving past this requires a coaching mindset of helping someone create a plan and then constantly sharing observations to help that person grow personally and professionally over time.

4. **Provide Greater Autonomy and Ownership:** A coach encourages team members to take ownership of their work, make decisions, and act independently. This can lead to a more engaged, motivated, and productive workforce and provide people the opportunity to develop critical thinking and problem-solving skills. Managers, in contrast, tend to take the lead on solving and resolving the most critical

issues, missing out on the chance to help someone develop the skill set to address the issue on their own and learn from the experience. It is important to openly acknowledge and discuss this tendency, as it is the only way to overcome a lack of autonomy and ownership that many people struggle with in most companies.

5. **Provide Real-Time Feedback:** Imagine a coach who only sits down with players once a year to let them know how they're doing. I certainly wouldn't want that person coaching my child. Every parent, and every child for that matter, would expect that coach to provide feedback during the game. The same is true in the workplace, where eight out of ten people prefer feedback in the moment.[28] Managers need to understand that they aren't doing their job if they aren't actively working with people every day to improve their performance and help them grow.

A shift in mindset from managing to coaching can drive major change for people individually and your company collectively. However, making this work requires another evolution in how we think—from evaluation to conversation. Without consistent and caring dialogue, coaching is nothing more than a concept. This is an extremely challenging transition for managers, as this evaluation mindset has been in place for over one hundred years. But it's worth a shot because the upside is enormous.

CHAPTER NINE

Evolve from Evaluation to Conversation

MINDSET SHIFT #4

Managing	→	COACHING
You Work for Me		We Work Together

Making the shift from *evaluation* to *conversation* has so much upside potential it is stunning. At the same time, it is also incredibly hard to overcome, as the traditional approach of how we evaluate people is so hard coded into everything that we do. Using evaluations has its place, but the way in which they are used is often misplaced and misguided. While conversation leads to collaboration, evaluation often leads to confrontation.

This happens in all areas of our life, both inside of work and outside of work as well. So, let's start there.

Our Evaluation Obsession

The moment we walk into a school for the first time, we begin to be evaluated. That measure begins to define us. Good grades mean you are smart; bad grades mean you aren't. That's how others begin to describe us, and it's how we begin to think of ourselves. This cloud hung over my head from an early age. I struggled with dyslexia in school. The words I heard and the looks I got from others told me who I was and what I wasn't.

But we learn later in life that there are different forms of intelligence; the ability to read, retain, and take a test is just one measure. Someone might be artistically gifted and incredibly creative or have incredible social skills and work exceptionally well with others. These are all incredibly important professional skills, but they wouldn't even register on a report card in a school setting. Also, a student may have challenges at home or be struggling with issues going on inside of them. None of these factors would be considered in a traditional grading system, yet working through hard things like this—learning to endure and overcome—is exactly what you need in someone who has to work through complex situations in the workplace. So, to be clear, it's not that grades aren't important, but it's critical to recognize that they're only one measure. They are not the complete definition or often even an accurate reflection of a person.

We have essentially carried over the same evaluation-based approach that we learned in school into the workplace. One example is that many companies evaluate managers based on an occasional employee engagement survey. This often puts managers on the defensive and in conflict with their team. Behind the scenes they react instinctively and start to sort through who they feel might have rated them low. This is not their fault; it's just human nature. If we don't want them to do this, we need to consider a different approach.

Instead, we should be focused on the actions managers are taking to drive improvements and if they're making progress over time. The only way to do this is to stop approaching employee experience as an anonymous evaluation and start turning it into a collaborative conversation. Once again, it's ingrained and very difficult to change, but when you take a step back and look at it objectively, there is a significant upside in finding ways to modify the approach.

Of course, we have also set up a system where employees are evaluated each year by their manager. Like a teacher, the manager grades that employee, but it's typically just one score at the end of the year; there aren't quizzes, papers, or tests to help someone understand where they stand over the course of the year like in school. And that annual grade, or performance review, carries a great deal of weight. It determines whether they get a raise and whether or not they get promoted or perhaps fired. While there are merits to this process, there are also significant flaws.

Most People Are Flying Blind

Most evaluations are primarily subjective, and while you can try to come up with some objective measures, they simply don't exist for many roles. Due to this reality, the main thing that's being evaluated is how someone did relative to expectations. So, it follows that clarity and alignment on expectations is the single most important thing that needs to happen. Yet it often doesn't.

Most employees are flying blind, and expectations are often unclear. The first issue was revealed in a Gallup survey where only one of four employees stated that their manager includes them in setting their goals.[29] That begins the disconnect. The second issue is that managers aren't able to provide clarity on expectations, often because you can only provide so much detail. There are nuances in most roles in most companies. But the biggest problem isn't the initial setting of goals or expectations, it's the lack of ongoing conversation. People aren't consistently told where they stand, especially when things aren't going well, because managers are more comfortable avoiding conflict. And of course, over time, challenges come up, and there may be things outside of someone's direct control that are going to affect their ability to make progress. Circumstances inevitably change over the course of the year, and it's critical to consider how to reset expectations. But often this doesn't happen because there is no formal process in place to instill this in most companies.

The only way to overcome these issues is to consistently have conversations where you confirm or refine expectations, share observations, and make changes. Employees who receive daily feedback from their manager are three times more likely to be engaged than people who have a more traditional, once- or twice-a-year review.[30] With that said, this consistent conversation with their manager simply doesn't happen for most people, but it can and it should.

The Grades Aren't Clear or Fair

The other major challenge is that the grading system companies use is often seen by people on their team as being unclear and unfair. It is critical for companies to embrace this reality and not try to wish it away or look for excuses. Facing this widespread perception head on is the only way to get past it.

One example of this is the rating system used by Meta, formerly known as Facebook. To be fair, their approach is not that different from most companies, but they have six levels of ratings: meets some expectations, meets most expectations, meets all expectations, exceeds expectations, greatly exceeds expectations, redefines expectations. The amount of time that it would take to train people on what those measures mean and the challenge of getting everyone to think about them consistently would be incredibly difficult for any company, even one with the resources and brainpower of Meta.

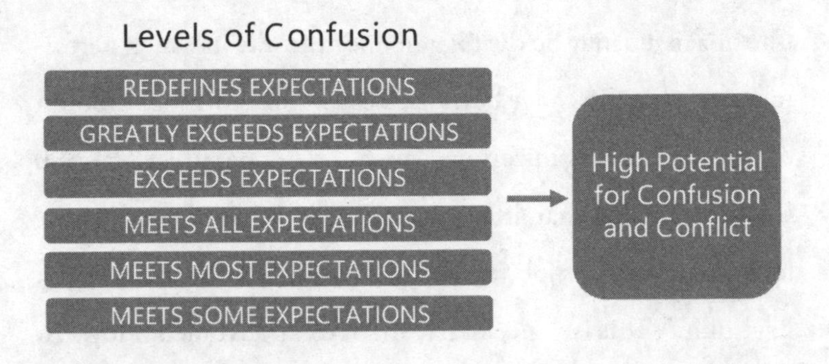

With that said, regardless of the definitions a company uses, there will be consistent inconsistencies as expectations differ between managers. What one may see as exceeding expectations may simply be meeting expectations to another manager, and neither is necessarily wrong. Also, while an employee may exceed expectations one year, the next year the expectations can and probably should be higher, and they may just meet them or fall short.

The good news is that this can be addressed, but it requires a radical rethinking and significant simplification of these definitions. And, of course, an honest evaluation of whether everyone is truly on the same page to ensure a level of fairness and consistency.

The Stress Is Significant

The final issue may be the biggest one. The way in which performance evaluations have been used causes an enormous amount of personal and organizational stress. An Adobe survey of 1,500 workers revealed that after a review, 37 percent of people have looked for another job, 22 percent have cried, and 20 percent have quit.[31] This isn't necessary, and it can be avoided. How? At its root, it's a design issue.

The review process for most companies is an annual evaluation followed by a formal discussion on three big things: someone's performance for the past year; their career and growth plan, which may include a potential promotion; and of course, a compensation review, including a raise and, potentially, a bonus if applicable. Because of this design, it's no surprise that the discussion on performance is the equivalent of a warm-up act, and the career conversation is often a sideshow. The main stage is clearly compensation. The end result is an annual process that's unintentionally designed to create conflict—and unfortunately, it hits that mark every year.

The intent here is not to address all of these design issues; there are opportunities for improvement across the board. The callout is to highlight how this design undermines the effectiveness of the evaluation and cuts the legs out from under the critical discussion around that person's career.

With that said, one year-end discussion isn't nearly enough when it comes to communicating expectations or coaching someone to help their career. It has to be a continuous conversation. So, let's get into how you can spark a shift in that direction.

Shifting Your Mindset from Evaluation to Conversation

Here are five steps you can take to *shift* the mindset of your company from evaluation to conversation:

1. **Create Coaching Conversations:** The key is to instill a process in your company that builds on and takes the pressure off the annual performance-evaluation process. One thing that leaders repeat as a mantra is that if managers are doing their job right, there should be no surprises in their performance evaluations. This implies an assumption that you're already having these conversations with members of your team and communicating any concerns on a consistent basis. The problem is that this expectation isn't always

clear to managers, and there is no process to ensure that it takes place. The way past this is to communicate clearly to the members of your management team an expectation that they are meeting with members of their team consistently for coaching conversations. And, based on their extensive research of millions of managers, Gallup has concluded that the single best habit of effective managers is having one fifteen- to thirty-minute conversation with each team member every week.[32] This approach creates a more collaborative, less intimidating, more timely, and more effective way to manage performance on an ongoing basis.

2. **Simplify the Performance Process:** The annual performance-review process is still important, but only if it is used effectively, and we change the mindset from evaluation to conversation. While the topic of the performance rating and review process is one that HR professionals are very passionate about, they're not big fans of it either. The solution is to do everything we can to clarify and simplify the process. This is not going to be easy, given the level of inertia. The good news is that there are options. As an example, I used an evaluation approach that had just three levels: exceeds expectations, meets expectations, and below

expectations. *Meets* is a great rating, as it means that I have high expectations and you hit them. *Exceeds* means you took your own initiative to do more, and the rating is my way of telling you that it's both recognized and appreciated. *Below* means that we have work to do together, and we need to collaborate to ensure the expectations are clear and progress is made. The key is that there is also an understanding that managers may not be communicating expectations, and the employees may not understand them. Using three simple levels helps to set that stage to have that critical conversation.

3. **Separate Performance, Compensation, and Career Conversations:** A simple step to open up and enhance conversations is to set up separate discussions for performance, career, and compensation, as they are very different topics. As we outlined, when all of these collide into a single discussion, the anxiety levels go up and conflict often follows. My personal approach was to always let people know that I would not use their rating to determine their raise or whether or not they were promoted. While I realize this runs counter to how many others approach this, consider the logic. Imagine a scenario where your

company shifts to self-evaluations—you are rating you. As I have high expectations for myself, if I had a good year, my honest self-evaluation would typically be "meets expectations." But the moment someone tells me that this rating might affect whether or not I get promoted, a raise, or a bonus, I am inclined to push for the highest rating possible. That simple example is the world we all live in. It's the essence of the issue and why it makes sense to consider decoupling this process.

4. **Create an Expectation of Collaboration:** Collaboration is the most essential ingredient in a productive relationship between a teacher and a student, a coach and a player, or a manager and an employee. This is something everyone needs to know if they want to grow. You can't tell someone to grow or make them grow; they have to be part of the process. The traditional one-way evaluation process runs counter to that, where someone feels like they are being evaluated when they receive feedback, judged when they acknowledge a weakness, and condemned when they share a concern. If you follow the path outlined in the actions above, you will make progress in overcoming these issues. Still, you may hit a wall if every person doesn't understand

that they are the owner of their own growth plan and the rest of us, including their manager, are just there to help. Having a great process and a great manager will only go so far in the same way that a great school and a great teacher can only do so much. If the student isn't interested and doesn't engage, they're not going to learn. Every leader and every manager should focus on instilling and ensuring that their relationship with their team members is a trusted and collaborative one. Creating that mindset can help reset relationships in a significant and substantive way.

5. **Instill Pride and Drive Progress:** One of the most important conversations you can have with members of your team relates to how they view their job and what it means to them. This may seem like a small thing, but instilling a sense of pride might be the biggest step you can take to create a positive and productive culture. Too often managers use the term *productivity* when what they should really be focused on is an individual's *output* and whether or not it is *meaningful* to the company, to you, and to the team member. That sense of purpose is essential to all of us, but managers rarely discuss it. The challenge for leaders is shifting our mentality from thinking like we're running

a factory, where the key metric is productivity, to ensuring that the output of each member of the team is truly meaningful to the company. The term that I like to use is "meaningful output." This gives the individual the ownership to drive the output but the manager the responsibility to make sure it is meaningful to the company and to that person. This creates a sense of pride for each person and a sense of connection to the broader company. Whatever metrics or approach you put in place, just make sure that they truly instill pride and drive progress.

In *STEP ONE: See the Shift* we outlined the forces of nature that have radically changed how we work. In *STEP TWO: Shift Your Mindset* we detailed the mindset shifts that are required to move your company forward. Our next step in *Holy Shift* is to make shift happen.

STEP THREE
Make Shift Happen

"If you want people to do something, make it easy."

Richard Thaler
Nobel Prize Winner and Founding Father of Behavioral Economics

THE PRINCIPLES, POLICIES, and procedures as well as the tools and tactics that have evolved over the last hundred years simply won't work for the next hundred years, much less the next ten.

For that reason, I considered calling this book *The Revenge of Common Sense* because it seems like we have lost our logic and our way regarding how we experience work. The good news is that everyone feels there's a better way to do things. Now it's time to give it a shot.

At the very least we need to get rid of the things that don't work and try something new. To quote a lyric from a song in the latest version of the movie *A Star Is Born*,

"Maybe it's time to let the old ways die."

We recently conducted research to see if the old ways were working. Our study covered companies of all sizes in every region of the country across fifteen industrial sectors.[33] The results were concerning.

Less than one in four people strongly agree that they feel a sense of pride and purpose in their work. And only one in ten strongly agree that they are excited to get out of bed in the morning and go to work. The end result, not surprisingly, is that close to one in three said that they are likely to leave their company in the next year.

Work Isn't Working

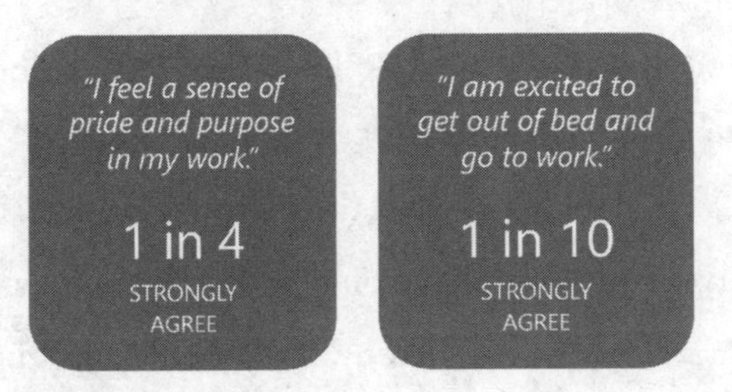

Clearly, it's "time to let the old ways die" and make shift happen. And the good news is we can, but we'll need to have a plan.

Creating a Plan That Is Evergreen for Your Team

In that spirit, in this section we'll share a fresh and pragmatic approach in the hope of helping to bring a sense of pride and purpose back to work. We'll provide a practical playbook that cuts through the clutter to radically simplify what we all now need to set in motion. But, in order to ensure your plan really hits the mark, any plays that you run will need to rest on top of a strategic framework that provides an evergreen, rock-solid foundation.

The word *evergreen* means that something is built to last, stays fresh, and is universally and continually relevant.[34] That's exactly what every company needs right now. The good news is that there is a proven way to do just that.

Having worked in public and private companies as well as in and around nonprofits, I consistently saw the same problem where CEOs couldn't explain their strategy or plan in a way that everyone on their team could both understand and internalize, much less be inspired by. They would introduce goals in a manner that was impossible for people to relate to—only to change their goals a few months later. But one day I found someone who had solved that problem, on the biggest stage and largest scale possible.

Healthcare is a $4 trillion industry. It touches every single person and has an absolutely endless number of big and complex problems. Back in 1994, Dr. William Kissick, a professor at the Wharton School of Business as well at the University of Pennsylvania School of Medicine, coined the term *Iron Triangle*, later called *The Triple Aim*, as a strategic framework for going after the three evergreen and "forever" problems that need to be solved in healthcare: access, quality, and cost.[35] Close to three decades later, this is still the framework used to focus efforts on improving the largest industry in our economy. The lesson learned—in order to get a large number of people focused on a problem over a long period of time, you need to simplify it and stick with it.

When I had the opportunity to become a CEO, I borrowed that concept and set three goals that I thought could be permanent. For the next ten years, we stuck to our version of *The Triple Aim*—serve, innovate, and separate. This strategy to serve our customers in a world-class manner, innovate by creating truly unique solutions, and separate ourselves from our competition, resulted in growing our bottom line by twenty times, or 2,000 percent, over that period of time. It worked.

We now need a simple and practical framework like this to help every company move forward to the future of work. So, here you go.

Getting to the CORE

In the spirit of the same simplicity as *The Triple Aim*, we are introducing *The CORE Four Framework.* It captures the four core components that are evergreen when it comes to your company culture. Each component applies to everyone on your team right now, as well as in the future, and drives the growth of people individually, as well as your company collectively. And pulling them together into a single strategic framework provides a formula to help create a company and a culture that is built to last.

In order to turn culture into a strategy that truly sets your company apart, the most critical thing has always been and will always be to help people to feel part of your "CORE." After all, the goal when it comes to culture shouldn't be to attain a score. It should be to get as many people on your team as possible to feel like they are in the flow and part of your CORE. That's how you create a world-class company culture because that's where people find pride and purpose and leaders build trust.

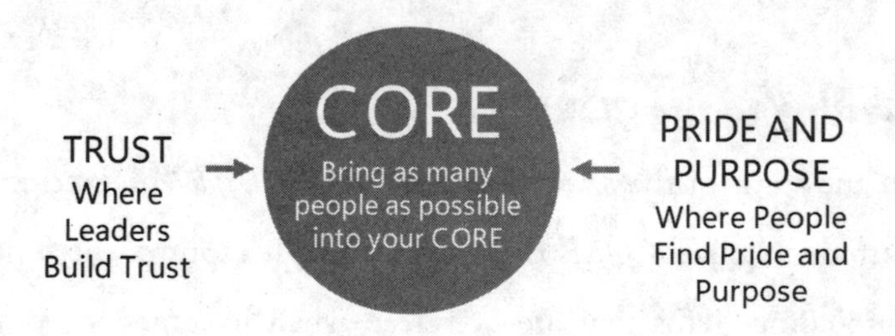

CORE is an acronym for Community, Opportunity, Relationships, and Experiences, the four factors that help bring people on your team into your inner CORE, where they feel truly connected to your company and their coworkers.

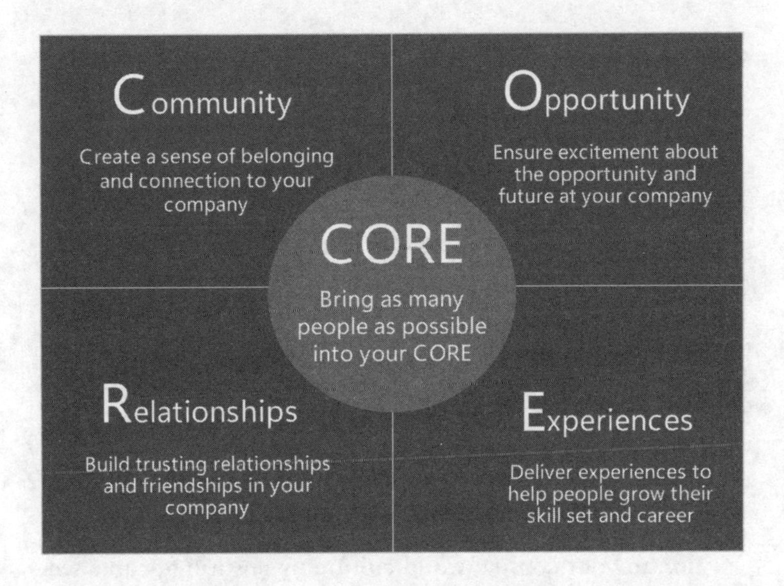

The four components of CORE are common sense, and all directly correlate with the three metrics that matter most to leaders—employee productivity, engagement, and retention.

1. **Community:** Creating a sense of belonging and connection to your company and culture.

2. **Opportunity:** Ensuring excitement about the future long-term opportunities at your company.

3. **Relationships:** Building trusting relationships and friendships in your company.

4. **Experiences:** Delivering experiences to help you grow your skill set and career.

Each component of CORE is focused on driving the growth of every member of your team, which is the fuel that drives the growth of your company over time. Each element of CORE falls into one of two categories based on whether it is culture-based or career-based:

- **Culture-Based:** The goal is to build a sense of connection to your company and culture by ensuring people feel a sense of belonging and helping them to build trusting relationships with others on the team. *(CORE Model Components: Community and Relationships)*

- **Career-Based:** The objective is to help build someone's individual career by providing clarity about future opportunities and experiences that help them to grow. *(CORE Model Components: Opportunity and Experiences)*

The four CORE components can also be broken out by where the ownership needs to be in order to drive and deliver the experience for members of the team:

- **Company-Driven:** The company owns putting the right processes, systems, and structures in place that build a sense of community and ensure people understand their future opportunities. *(CORE Model Components: Community and Opportunity)*
- **Manager-Driven:** The manager owns helping team members build connections and relationships as well as ensuring that they have experiences that help them grow. *(CORE Model Components: Relationships and Experiences)*

STEP THREE: Make Shift Happen takes you through each component of *The CORE Four Framework*, providing you with both a strategy and a post-pandemic playbook that you can leverage to move your company forward.

"The CORE Four Framework" for Moving Your Company Forward

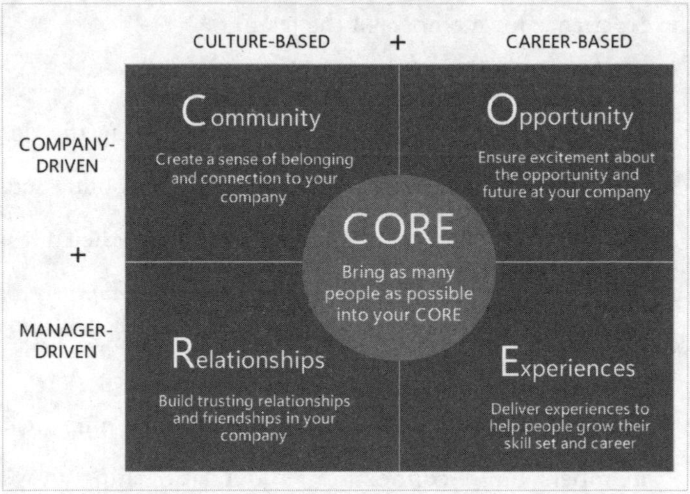

CULTURE-BASED + CAREER-BASED

COMPANY-DRIVEN + MANAGER-DRIVEN

Community
Create a sense of belonging and connection to your company

Opportunity
Ensure excitement about the opportunity and future at your company

CORE
Bring as many people as possible into your CORE

Relationships
Build trusting relationships and friendships in your company

Experiences
Deliver experiences to help people grow their skill set and career

The plays that are outlined apply to companies in every setting—office, remote, and hybrid—and are relevant to every person and every company, regardless of size, industry, or location. And the framework provides you with a strategy that is evergreen—the four components of CORE have always been, and will always be, at the center of the bull's-eye and the very heart of what truly matters.

We all want and need to feel like we're part of the CORE and feel a sense of pride and purpose in our work. Great leaders are real-life action figures who can make that happen. Everything in this strategic framework and practical playbook is an action that has the potential to make work better for every member of your team. Let's start with the first component of *The CORE Four Framework*—COMMUNITY.

CHAPTER TEN

COMMUNITY—Drive Connection to Company and Culture

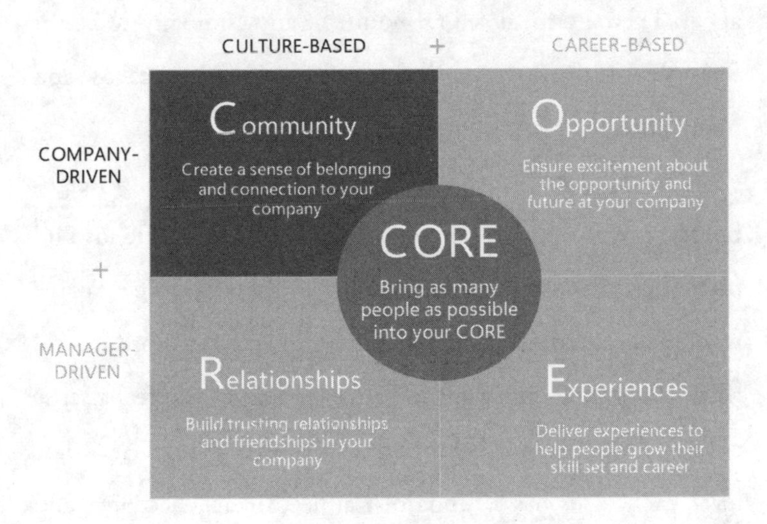

Creating a sense of community is the first and most important shift you need to make happen in order to turn culture into a strategy at your company. Without it you don't have a company culture, which is exactly what most companies are struggling with right now. It's a bigger problem than you may think.

In our research, only one out of every five people strongly agree that they feel a sense of belonging at their company and a sense of connection to their company culture. That's far too low because simply stated—no community, no culture.

We All Want to Belong

A true sense of belonging and feeling part of a larger group has always been a critical selling point for any company. When it doesn't exist, the door is wide open for someone to leave—and many have.

In the same way that it's hard to move out of a neighborhood or leave a school where you have lots of friends and memories, that same concept applies to the workplace. People want to and need to feel like they are connected to those around them. They don't just want to be in a group, but to feel a sense of connection to and belonging within that group. At a base level, each of us has a fundamental need to feel accepted and respected. In many ways, it's that simple.

According to a 2022 BCW survey of 13,000 workers, companies that prioritized an inclusive environment increased their retention rate by 24 percent.[36] One of the critical points in the report was that,

> *"Organizations that ignore workplace culture do so at their peril; when just one of the most important workplace culture needs isn't met—such as open and honest communication, sense of belonging and feeling valued, visible leadership, or focus on well-being—the number of employees saying they are very likely to stay in their current job drops to 39%."*

That said, creating that sense of community and a sense of connection with your company and with coworkers is now more challenging than ever. We are not together in the same way we used to be, and even when we are, it feels different because we have changed. It's time to create a new approach that acknowledges the shifts that have taken place. One that is focused on what's most important. It starts with creating a community.

Creating a Community

The definition of a community is "a group of people within a common characteristic living within a larger society." And there is another, similar version that applies to the workplace: "A body of persons of common and especially professional interests scattered in a larger society."[37]

There are two consistent terms in these definitions. The first is the word "common," not surprising, as the root of the word *community* is derived from the Latin word *communis,* which means common. Understanding this is critical, as it provides the exact roadmap that we need to follow to rebuild culture in companies. Simply stated, the more we have in common and the deeper those connections are, the stronger the community. That concept applies to all of us, personally and professionally.

If you don't have anything in common with others, and the things that you do don't matter to at least a few in the group, then you don't have a community. This has always been a major challenge for companies. Most struggle to translate their vision, mission, and values into something that matters to people on a personal level. The default solution has been to bring everyone together in the same office, or off-site for an all-hands meeting, and hope that these terms sink in with people over time. That approach was, at times, effective, but it always had limits.

I teach a graduate class in a business school where all of

the students also work full-time. Every semester I ask them to write down the vision, mission, and values of their current company, without looking them up. No one has been able to do it. More importantly, it is pretty clear that those words don't mean much to them. They are not alone. Most employees at any company would fail this test and so would their leaders. I have held workshops with executives where I ask them to repeat those things for their company, and none of them could do it. So, while those guardrails are critical for every company, maybe they aren't what actually creates your culture, which brings us to that second term.

The second term that is consistent in both definitions of *community* is "in a larger society." It acknowledges that communities are actually just subgroups within a larger group. Once again, this is true in both our personal and professional lives. We may live in the same area as ten thousand people, but only form meaningful relationships with fewer than ten of them. And even if we went to a college with fifty thousand people, we are probably only close to a handful of people a few years later.

The same is true at work. The place where culture really comes together has always been in smaller groups formed within a larger organization. These groups could be people who have the same role, tenure, or desk location, or who work on the same team or project together. Or maybe it is on a more personal level, and they are the same age, have the same background, or share the same interests. In other words, they have something in common. These communities formed somewhat naturally in the past. Now that we are more scattered and work in a more distributed fashion, we have to be more intentional in helping to form these communities.

Moving forward, the challenge for every leader is understanding that creating a single, top-down macro approach will not work anymore. This was the culture play that I ran for the last twenty years in building high-growth, high-performing companies, but it's no longer going to work. Again, don't get me wrong. Thoughtful top-down principles like vision, mission, and values still need to be in place, and all-hands meetings can be helpful. But to make shift happen, your focus must evolve from the company overall to the experience of each individual person and the people around them.

The good news is that communities have always existed and will always exist within larger societies. So there is a way to approach bringing people together that can and will work. We just have to be more deliberate in our approach. The great news is that there are many ideas that you can deploy right now to help move your company forward.

Community: Make Shift Happen

Here are five actions you can set in motion to create a sense of belonging and connection to your company:

1. **Drive Connection with Your Campus:** One of the best ways to help your company and team move forward is to simply change your terminology and tactics. To help spark a new way of thinking, when I was CEO of our five-hundred-person company, we stopped using the term *office* and made the shift to calling it a *campus*, similar to a college campus. A student goes to campus for classes, group projects, and events. But they can get their work done anywhere at any time. They don't need to go to a library to study any more than we need to go to an office to do independent, focused work, whether it is writing code or a research report. We can start thinking of an office, or campus, in the same way. Clearly communicating the purpose of your space and how you intend to use it to help foster a sense of connection is a simple step in the right direction. Pivoting from an

office-based model to a campus-based approach communicates a more positive and forward-thinking message. The key is to use your campus to create purpose-driven events and experiences that foster a strong sense of community in your company.

2. **Host Management Collaboration Weeks:** One very effective step that many companies are taking to foster communities is bringing different subgroups together. In my last company, over half of our team was located out of state, making it difficult to create a strong community among our management team. An approach that we used, which worked extremely well, was bringing all managers to our main campus every ninety days for a week of meetings covering four domains: business review, product roadmap review, functional review, and key initiatives review. The ten members of our executive leadership team would sit in a half circle with the presenter in front. Every meeting was open and optional for every member of the broader management team. This accomplished two critical things—visibility for the presenters and transparency for everyone on the team. This approach helped to build trust within, among, and across the management team. By

having everyone in town for a few days, with time slots open to set their own meetings, as well as facilitated get-togethers, everyone felt like they were part of a community.

3. **Create Cohorts:** Fostering micro communities is essential. A great way to make this happen is by creating cohorts. Cohorts are groups of five to eight people within or across teams, which create a sense of connection with others on the team and a sense of belonging across the company. Cohorts can be formed based on when people start, such as a new-hire class, or on common interests or experience levels. The key is to make people feel part of a group, and the easiest place to start is with something that they have in common. The best practice is to encourage cohorts outside of your direct team, as this provides a connection to a broader set of people across the company. This is needed and necessary at every level of the organization, from executive to entry-level roles. When I was first given the chance to lead a company, I was pretty lost and alone. The role itself is very insular and isolating. To help address and alleviate that, I joined an organization called YPO and formed a cohort with eight other CEOs. For over ten years, we have met once a month for four hours. This

may sound like a huge commitment of time, but it is a standard process that has been in place for decades and is used by over 30,000 leaders in over one hundred countries across the world, because it works. And it was the single most impactful investment in my growth over that decade. This same type of model, where you form cohorts based on something people have in common, can and should be used in every company. It doesn't have to be that same time commitment, but bringing a cohort of people together consistently is a proven way to help create strong micro communities in any setting.

4. **Invest in Company Retreats and Events:** One of the big challenges with cutting back on real estate is that once you accrue the savings, that becomes your new normal, and anything you spend now feels incremental. We touched on this earlier: the dangers of removing budget items permanently that were only temporary savings. For example, if you save $400,000 per year on space by going completely virtual, and then spend $100,000 flying everyone in, getting them a hotel room and investing in a company meeting, you tend not to view the $300,000 as savings over the previous year but as a $100,000 hit in the

current year. For that reason, it is best to bake investments in bringing your team together into your baseline budget every year as an immovable object. The amount of money in the example is equivalent to one FTE, a small price to pay for helping members of your team feel connected to your company. It is important to recenter our mindset that this type of investment should be a standard. At the same time, we also need to make sure to maximize the impact of that investment. The focus should be on building relationships and your community, not on training, which can be done virtually. The key is to focus the time on things that can only be done when you are together in person.

5. **Conduct a Vision, Mission, and Values Workout:** One of the mistakes that we all make is assuming that people understand and internalize our vision, mission, and values. The reality is that most of the time those things don't connect with the people on our team because we don't take the time to personalize them. To help get past this, you can conduct a "workout" with members of your team. In advance of any session, have each member of your team write down how your company's vision, mission and values relate to them personally. It is critical to encourage

candor and be supportive of any team member who doesn't connect with any one or all of them. This feedback, even if negative, is your opening for a deeper and more meaningful discussion. Based on what people write down, you can then review with each employee individually or facilitate a group discussion. In most companies it is likely that a number of employees won't initially feel a connection. That is normal and expected. Your goal is to help them connect the dots by exploring their personal connection as well as by explaining how their role supports and aligns with your company's vision, mission, and values.

Setting a strategy in motion to create communities within your company will strengthen the inner core of your company. The next step is to ensure that everyone on the team understands and is excited about being part of the company and the future. Surprisingly, this is the one area that companies miss the most and it is the second component of *The CORE Four Framework*—OPPORTUNITY.

CHAPTER ELEVEN

OPPORTUNITY—Ensure Excitement about the Future

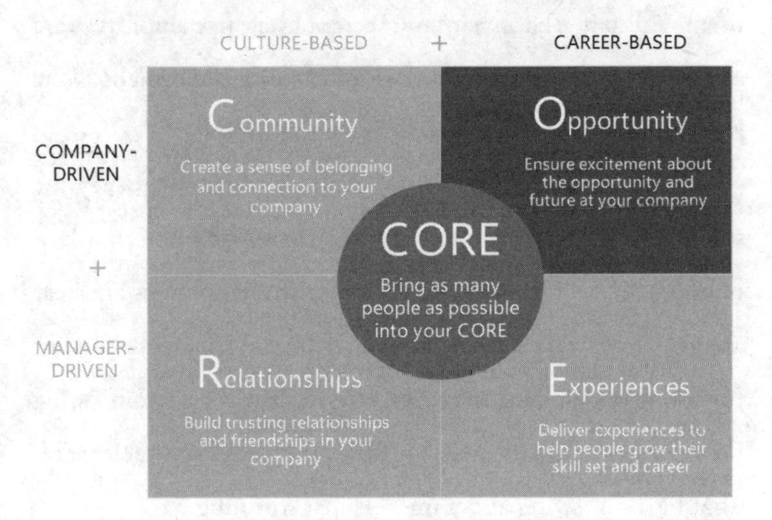

You might have heard the saying, "hope is not a strategy." Well, in the case of how someone feels about their future, hope is actually *the* strategy. When someone doesn't have hope, they will turn inward and regress instead of turning outward and progressing in their life as well as in their career. If someone doesn't feel like they have a future at your company, they likely have one foot out of the physical or proverbial door already. And the bad news for every leader in every company is that you may be the one who is opening it for them.

In our research, we found that only one out of every five people strongly agree that they feel like they have a future at the company and can see the long-term opportunities ahead of them within it. That means four out of every five employees are at some level of risk because lack of career advancement is the number one reason why people leave their job.

In fact, three out of every four employees say they are somewhat or very likely to leave their company due to a lack of opportunity.[38] Yet only one of every two employees are clear about their career path. So, while it's the single biggest cause of turnover, leaders and managers aren't clearly communicating the next step in their career to half of the people on their team. That big of a "swing and a miss" is just stunning.

When you ask employees at high risk of exiting a company why they want to leave, seven of every ten say they need to leave the organization to advance their career.[39] Just think of the phrase people use when they switch jobs; they say the left for another "opportunity." The action for every leader is making sure the employee sees that next opportunity within your company.

I learned the hard way that it's not as easy as it sounds. While as a company we were pretty good at communicating an engaging mission and building a world-class culture, not surprisingly we still had people leave. To counter this, I put a protocol in place for a period of time. When anyone resigned, our team had to set up a meeting with me and the employee in the next twenty-four hours to try to turn them around. While I was able to convince a few folks along the way to stay, I'm sure you can imagine how this approach made everyone feel. Clearly the CEO of the company shouldn't be stepping in.

The right move is to create an ongoing process where conversations and clarity about someone's future happen before they decide to leave. And it should be an ongoing collaboration between that person and their manager, not the leader of the company. People need to consistently have conversations about where the company is heading as well as where they are heading from a career perspective. Some think of this as being clear on someone's next move on the career ladder, but that has become an outdated concept. Many companies are now moving to a more realistic and, in many ways, optimistic approach to career progression.

The big shift in motion in terminology and tactics is away from a career *path* and towards a career *lattice*. A career path is linear, while a career lattice allows for movement up and across the organization.

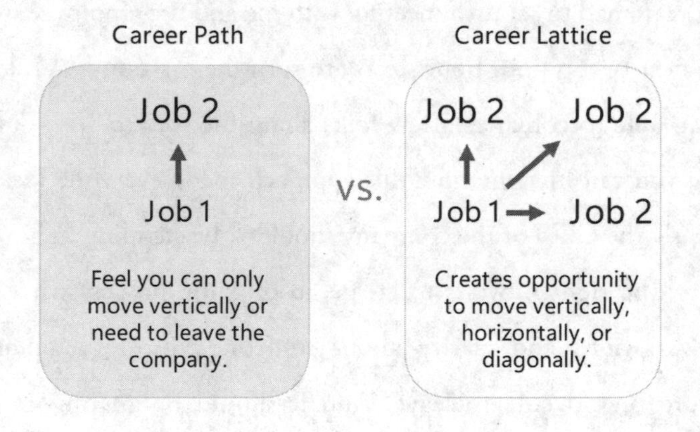

Creating a career lattice is a great way to ensure that everyone on your team understands both how they can progress and the many potential opportunities ahead of them in the future. Lattices show an employee how they can move within their current role and function, as well as how they can progress to other functions and roles within your company. A lattice is not a job description. Instead, it outlines competencies and behaviors that can be observed or measured, which represent success in each role. As roles progress, a lattice clarifies how behaviors and competencies evolve. It helps set the stage for someone to build a career at your company versus just do their job.

With that said, there is also a need to create more customized development plans for people. A few decades ago, many grade schools began developing IEPs, or individual education plans, to map each student's progress and help chart their course from one school year to another. The idea was to customize a student's journey rather than just assign them letter grades and pass them up to the next level.

Applying this to the business world, there is a critical need to extend our focus from just providing job training for a specific role to creating a true individual development plan for each member of your team. In a Gallup survey of 15,000 workers, 65 percent stated that learning new skills is an extremely or very important factor in deciding whether to leave for a new job, and 61 percent said it was extremely or very important in deciding whether to stay at their current company.[40]

Whether you use a lattice, individual development plan or some other tool is not the point. What's most critical is that every leader and manager ensure that each member of their team clearly understands their next step and how they can grow and develop at your company. Even though that sounds simple, it is exceptionally rare to have a manager who actively nurtures and cares about someone's career. That's why it is so crucial to create a process that instills this as a standard for your team. It can and will have a major impact on where your company goes from here.

Opportunity: Make Shift Happen

Here are five actions you can set in motion to help ensure excitement about the future and the long-term opportunities at your company:

1. **Consider Career Lattices:** As outlined earlier, career lattices are an incredibly effective way to clearly communicate the level of opportunity for someone at your company. Even if you are a small company, you can set this principle in motion just by communicating that you are flexible and open to someone's future interests and supportive of their movement across the company. Each manager should

spend time with team members using a lattice or some other tool to outline opportunities for growth, as well as the competencies and behaviors they have to demonstrate. This opens up the dialogue on an employee's career path and shows how you, as their manager, can partner to support their career development. That's what every employee wants and needs.

2. **Encourage Lateral Career Moves:** While having a career lattice or a similar tool in place is an important step, it won't get you anywhere if you don't have an organizational ethos of encouraging lateral career moves. Many people exit an organization because they feel that the person above them is never going to leave. An additional issue is that managers don't want to lose anyone, so they are often reluctant to encourage someone to explore other opportunities in the organization. For these reasons, moves across functions and teams, versus solely focusing on promotions, have to be encouraged and embraced by the entire management team. Managers need to have discussions with team members about career interests and desired skills, even if that entails moving to another team, and determine how they can best support their development. Whether it is

promotion within their team or a transition to another, managers should emphasize that the employee first needs to prove themselves in their current role. While managers may have some concerns that a conversation about moving to another team may lead to them losing someone, the reality is that they would likely lose them anyway. Employees who have made an internal move in their first two years with a company are 20 percent more likely to stay in the long-term.[41] At the same time, only 15 percent of employees say that their organization encouraged them to move to a new role. Taking a proactive approach to have this conversation will help increase overall retention for your company and trust within your team.

3. **Create a Development Plan for Each Team Member:** While group training programs are helpful, they aren't always available in every company, applicable to every employee, or accessible when someone needs them. For this reason, many companies are creating individualized development plans for members of their team. The good news is that, while the cost of training programs may be a budgetary constraint, there is an endless supply of free learning tools online. That reality can be overwhelming for

many people. The key is to help members of your team target the right tools. You can create a custom plan, leveraging company resources, and augment them with free tools, such as podcasts, TED Talks, or YouTube videos. Most leaders would tell you that they have learned through experience, school, conversations with their peers, and an endless number of articles, books, and conferences. And no two leaders would have the same list or the ability to recreate their own complete list for you. This is why it's important to inspire people to take action—read a book, listen to a podcast, attend a conference, meet with a peer—in order to develop that instinct and build that muscle over time. The key is to set something in motion. Per the LinkedIn study cited earlier, only 14 percent of people say that their organization encouraged them to build a career development plan. We all learn in different ways; the key is targeting the learning to each employee, creating a specific goal and commitment, such as completing one output every month, and then taking the time to discuss their development and growth.

4. **Leverage a Rolling Approach for Individual Goals:** One of the biggest breakthroughs that I've been involved in

during my career is moving away from annual goals for everybody in a company and shifting to more of a rolling approach. While setting annual targets is critical for hitting an overall plan at a company level, it doesn't translate to an individual level. The work of most team members doesn't fit into a twelve-month target. Often after sixty or ninety days, what was in someone's individual plan has already been accomplished or is no longer relevant. A rolling approach is a very effective way to address the shortcomings of annual goal setting. In a rolling approach, you revisit and refine goals at a regular cadence throughout the year. As the year progresses, some goals may have already been accomplished, and others may become unrealistic due to circumstances out of your control. A rolling approach gives you the ability to recalibrate throughout the year, creating a better and more grounded conversation. It also provides people with a greater sense of accomplishment on a more consistent basis. One approach that works well is to simply review the last thirty or ninety days and the accomplishments against an individual's goals, and then refine the goals as well as the targeted deliverables or outputs for the next thirty or ninety days. The key is to be open to refining, reprioritizing, and replacing the goal if necessary. This helps you raise the bar as well as remove what's no longer relevant.

5. **Create a Process to Showcase and Recognize Employees:** If you really want members of your team to get excited about their future at your company, one of the best things you can do is create a process for showcasing employees. While many companies may feel like they do this, most efforts fall short in terms of impact and reach. Company leaders often provide this opportunity for only a handful of employees and it doesn't happen often enough. The way forward is to put systems and processes in place that make recognition super simple. That can come via applications that enable employee recognition, but you can also just bake recognition into the way in which you get together as an organization. Examples include carving out time at the beginning of your team meetings for shoutouts and providing time for rapid-fire recognition when you have all-hands meetings. There are also simple things that every manager can do for team members, such as setting up a few minutes with a senior leader, or sending a note of recognition to the employee and copying members of

senior leadership. This combination of consistent peer-to-peer and senior management recognition will have a significant impact on how someone feels about their future with your company.

One of the most effective ways to increase retention and engagement is by ensuring that each member of the team understands and is excited about their future at your company. But in order to maintain this energy over time, it all comes down to trust. Which leads us to the next component of *The CORE Four Framework*—RELATIONSHIPS.

CHAPTER TWELVE

RELATIONSHIPS—Build Trust and Strengthen Teams

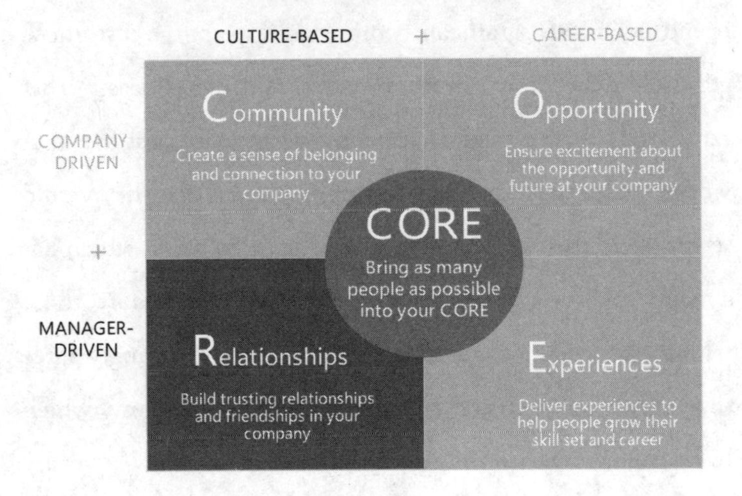

THE THREE MOST IMPORTANT words in real estate are location, location, and location. One could argue that the three most important words for creating a successful company or building a successful career are relationships, relationships, and relationships. And while relationships with customers, partners, investors, and other key stakeholders are critical, they all hinge on the strength of the relationships that built within your company. This is an area of risk for many companies. Our research revealed that only one in five people strongly agree that they have trusted relationships and many friends at their company.

The case for focusing on relationships as a core part of your strategy is an easy one to make. A recent Gallup study outlined the benefits. Employees who say they have a best friend at work are significantly more likely to engage customers, get more done in less time, innovate, and share ideas.[42] That same study also revealed that people who have a best friend at work are also twice as likely to strongly agree that they would recommend their company as a great place to work, which has a major impact on recruiting and retention. What's more, those with a best friend at work are twice as likely to strongly agree that they are extremely satisfied with their company, which has a major impact on productivity. A study by the University of Pennsylvania and the University of Minnesota showed that groups that had close and trusting relationships performed significantly better in decision making because of a greater degree of commitment and cooperation within the group.[43]

With that said, as we have shared, the most important relationship is the one a team member has with their manager. Our experience at work is primarily driven by this one-to-one relationship. So while building relationships across the company is critical, it won't matter much if someone isn't in a positive place with their manager. All of these data points taken together tell one clear story—relationships matter.

Every leader understands that if you want to build a business that will thrive in the long-term, nothing will have a bigger impact than the strength and depth of your relationships with your customers. After all, your reputation as a company is nothing more than a reflection of how your customers relate to your brand, product, and team.

Leaders also instinctively understand that relationships within their company are what drives collaboration and innovation and that these relationships and the sense of belonging that they create define, strengthen, and solidify your culture. The challenge is creating a strategy that helps facilitate relationship building for every person in the company. The good news is that if you can effectively address this, it's a win-win, as relationships are not only crucial to the company, they're also the most critical catalyst in everyone's career.

The Key Catalyst in Your Career

The impression you make on others and the relationships that you build have an enormous impact on both your professional growth and career. If you had only one career hack, this would be it.

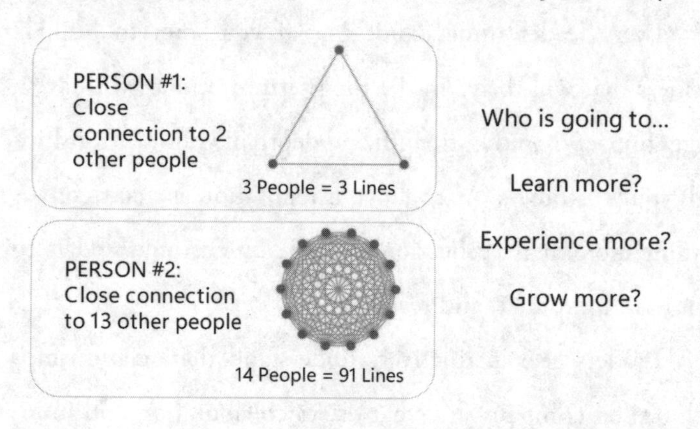

Simply stated, the more connections someone has at their company, the more they're going to learn, experience, and grow. But while deep, meaningful relationships are clearly critical to your career, no one teaches you or helps you nurture the skill and the substance of building relationships. And even though the trust that a leader builds with their team and their customers is also one of the most important things in running a company, there's very little, if any, leadership training dedicated to this skill.

As I shared, I interviewed every single person we hired in my decade as a CEO at my last company and also did an exit interview with every single person who left. In all cases—a data set of well over 1,000 interviews—the one thing everybody said consistently was that the most impressive thing about the company was the people they met and/or worked with. The fact that this may not seem surprising should tell you something.

There's an old saying that when someone looks back at their life, they never say, "I wished I spent more time at work." The implication is that they sacrificed time with their family and friends for their jobs. Along those same lines, when people look back on their careers, they all say that there is one thing that they treasure the most about work— the relationships that they built.

The fact that we don't teach the art and science of how to connect with others and build trusting relationships is a huge miss. Post-pandemic proximity challenges have made this even more difficult, so a formal focus on this is critical for companies.

Especially at the senior level, so much of building a team

comes down to trust. When you choose someone to join your team, how well you connect with that person and how much confidence you have in their references and reputation really matters. In that light, both good as well as bad relationships impact your career, so it's important to focus on both. While it is tough to work through the bad relationships that you'll inevitably encounter throughout your career, effectively addressing those awkward and tense situations is one of best tests of true leadership. In my own experience, whether it was a tough situation with a colleague or customer, I've learned to lean in. Some of those relationships are now my strongest ones.

I've participated in thousands of performance reviews and promotion discussions. The big reveal is that the conversation is about the *person* as much as it is about their *performance*. There is just no denying the fact that the impression that someone makes on others is a major factor in deciding whether or not to promote someone or give them a raise. That's the reality that many ignore at their own peril. Performance is and will always be a combination of objective and subjective measures. There are, of course, cases where a job is singular and isolated, and the person doesn't interact with others at all, but those are rare.

Putting all professional considerations aside, including your enjoyment of work, the most compelling case for building strong relationships is what it means to all of us personally.

The Harvard Study of Adult Development followed 724 men and more than 1,300 of their children over three decades.[44] This study used thousands of questions and hundreds of metrics to derive the secret to being healthy and happy. There was one constant that closely correlated with leading a good life. Can you guess? It turns out that the key to happiness is having good relationships. The authors also cited research that loneliness is twice as unhealthy as obesity and increases the probability of death in a given year by 26 percent. When we think about the health of our employees, that's a striking statistic to consider. And the long-term benefits are just as stunning. People who reported having the most satisfying relationships when they were age fifty were also healthier mentally and physically when they turned eighty.

That said, connecting with others doesn't come naturally for everyone. It certainly didn't for me. When I was growing up, I was somewhat of a recluse. It was a defense mechanism because I knew that if I avoided people, they couldn't hurt me. I didn't trust anyone and was very distant, even from those who were close to me. When it came to meeting new people, I had extreme anxiety. Over time, I grew out of it as I began to understand that the nature of relationships is actually pretty simple. It's a pattern and a process. And it all starts with being curious and figuring out what we have in common.

The Simple Science of Building Relationships

For the last 200,000 years, since the beginning of human history, people have built relationships based on two things: understanding what two people have in common on the surface, and then diving deeper and sharing common experiences to get to substance. Think of *surface* as what brings us together and *substance* as what keeps us together.

The base of the word relationship is the word *relate*. So the first step in getting to know someone when you're at that surface level is uncovering what you have in common. Doing so creates a foundation of trust and an invitation to dive deeper to discover your differences. When you are a kid, that can be as simple as having the same favorite color or superhero. When you are a teenager it might be the same activity, team, or favorite artist. When we get older it might be whether we have the same hobbies, went to the same school, live in the same area, cheer for the same teams, or have children who are the same age.

Think of it like a Venn Diagram waiting to happen. At first, every two people in this world are two separate circles. But all it takes are a few questions to uncover what we have in common. In other words, we truly "meet" in the middle; that's where it all starts.

The Simple Science of Building Relationships

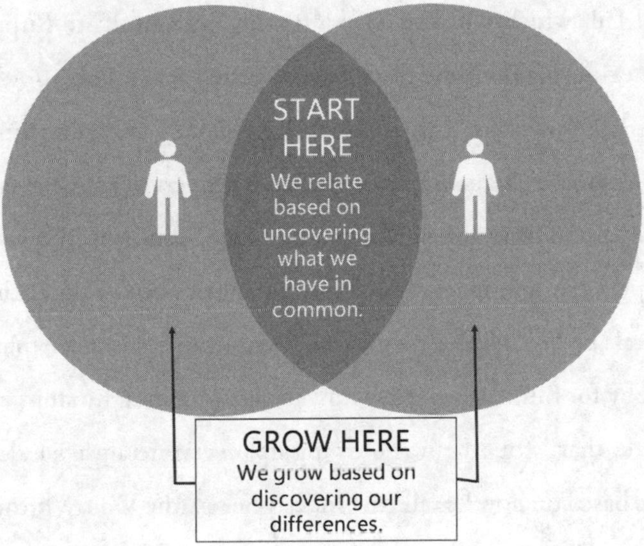

START HERE
We relate based on uncovering what we have in common.

GROW HERE
We grow based on discovering our differences.

Over time, we go below the surface to substance, which is where meaningful relationships get built. This requires diving deeper to discover our differences, learn new perspectives, and have new experiences, which is exactly where and how we grow.

But it all starts with uncovering what we have in common. And that only requires two things—curiosity and questions.

There is a wonderful episode in the first season of the series *Ted Lasso* that hit the center of the bull's-eye regarding why it's so critical to be curious. In the show, Ted is an American college football coach who is hired to coach an English Premier League soccer team by Rebecca, the team's owner. She is hoping Ted will fail, which will help her infuriate and humiliate Rupert, her ex-husband, as the team was his prized possession.

In one scene in this episode, Ted makes a bet with Rupert on a game of darts in the local pub. If Rupert wins, he gets to pick the starting lineup for the next two games. If Ted wins, Rupert can no longer come into the owner's box. Rupert then reveals he brought his own darts, indicating this is more than a hobby for him. When Ted's turn to throw comes, he stops and shares that, when he was growing up, everyone always judged him based on how he talked. One day he saw the Walt Whitman quote: "Be curious, not judgmental." This made Ted realize everything others said about him had nothing to do with him; it was about them. That epiphany changed everything. He then told Rupert that if he was curious, he might have asked Ted if he had played a lot of darts. And he would have said, "Yes, sir, every Sunday afternoon in a sports bar with my father, from age ten to sixteen, when he passed away." With that hanging in the air, Ted throws his final dart and hits the center of the bullseye, drawing cheers from others gathered around and tears from everyone watching the show, including me.

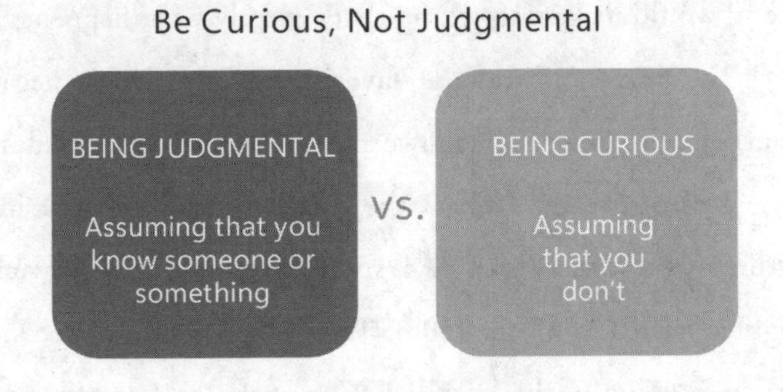

When you ask people what their favorite episode from the many seasons of *Ted Lasso* is, they all point to this scene. Why? Because no one wants to feel like they are being judged, but we've all felt it. It's universal. And that's why the essence of getting to know someone is so simple. It's about being curious. And all it takes is a few good questions.

There is an exercise I did one evening when I was going to graduate school that completely floored me. The class was taught by Dr. Joel Whalen, a former radio disc jockey. He had both the voice and the quirkiness you would imagine, but also an enormous passion and talent for teaching the art and science of communication. He was the best teacher I've ever had.

There were two sets of questions that he asked us that night. He said the first set of questions would make us laugh, the second would make us cry. And that's exactly what happened.

The first topic was our favorite holiday. People began shouting out answers. Halloween was shouted the loudest, so he probed deeper. "What's the craziest, most embarrassing costume you ever wore?" As students gave their answers, laughter started to fill the room. Then he pivoted. The second topic was going to the hospital. When was the last time you were there for family or a friend? Who were you there to see? Do you remember walking into the hospital? The sounds? The smell? Did you have tears in your eyes when you walked into the room?

The room got quieter as those questions turned more personal. The professor was right. His first set of questions made us laugh, and his second set had brought tears to many of our eyes, including mine.

The revelation is that asking questions in the right way at

the right time can move us from surface to substance, leading to deeper connections that help people feel heard, seen, and valued. Questions are powerful, and they are the key to building relationships. It all starts with being curious.

This simple, straightforward, and significant need to connect exists in every person and in every business. It's time to apply the right level of rigor and resources.

Relationships: Make Shift Happen

Here are five actions you set in motion to help build trusting relationships and friendships in your company:

1. **Create a Buddy System:** Mentor programs are good in concept, but they often aren't effective. Many companies are now moving to "buddy programs," where you assign everyone on your team a peer from either within their team or across the company. In contrast to a mentor program, these connections are between peers who are experiencing similar challenges and can provide ground-level guidance. Because they are peers, the relationship is easier to develop. Microsoft piloted a new-hire buddy program and found that the more the onboarding buddy met with the new

hire, the greater the new hire's perception of their own speed to productivity.[45] Fifty-six percent of new hires who met with their onboarding buddy at least once in their first ninety days indicated that their buddy helped them to quickly become productive in their role. That percentage increased to 97 percent for those who met more than eight times in their first ninety days. To help your buddy program succeed, ask people to participate who are solid role models. Attributes include someone who is respected by their peers and is a strong overall contributor to the company.

2. **Get Personal:** As we've detailed, meaningful relationships won't form without a deeper connection. There are a number of approaches that you can use to help people on your team get to know each other on a more personal level. This can only be done if the leader begins to open up and provides a safe space for others, but there are many creative ways to help set this in motion. You can have a "photo album" exercise where everyone shares one picture that is meaningful to them and tells the backstory that goes with it. Or have everyone share their "origin story" about growing up or about their family and where they came from. You can give people the chance to talk about causes

that are personal to them—a great way to spark potential efforts in the community for your team. If you want to try something extraordinarily powerful, just ask about a moment, person, or event that changed the course of their life. You will be amazed at how simple exercises like these can help pull people together.

3. **Level Up Your One-on-One:** The time you spend with someone one-on-one is the single biggest lever you have to build trust as a leader or manager. With that said, most miss using their one-on-one meetings as an opportunity to dive deeper and build more meaningful relationships with members of their team. To solve this, it is important to be intentional, and there are a number of ways to make this happen. The first is to allow your team members to own the meeting and provide the agenda in advance. Yes, *they* set the agenda. You can add topics to the list, but giving them control demonstrates your confidence in them. Begin the meeting by slowing down and asking something personal in an authentic and caring way, as this is essential in building trust and understanding. Initially focus on their items on the agenda, not yours. Listen actively and ask probing questions. Don't let things get off track with

too many details on open items and project updates unless that is explicitly the purpose of the meeting. And ensure that your next meeting includes a status check on the items from your last meeting. Instilling a standard process in your company will ensure that people feel heard professionally and seen personally, significantly enhancing this critical relationship with their manager.

4. **Create Common Connections:** Finding common connections between members of your team is the single biggest accelerant of relationships. This is low-hanging fruit that very few companies leverage effectively. In the past, this may have happened organically, but with the workforce more spread out, we now have to be more intentional. We truly don't know what we have in common with the person sitting next to or across from us unless it is somehow shared. That took some effort when we were in the same room or worked in the same building five days a week, but now it requires an entirely different approach. I have led group and company exercises over the last few years where we poll the group on both professional and personal questions. People are always amazed that there are others just like them, right next to them. One idea is

to apply the concept of *circles,* which we explored earlier. Creating common connections is most critical in the circle that represents the daily, ongoing reality for each team member. That circle defines their experience at your company because it is the context in which they do their job, interact with coworkers, and engage with their manager. It's critical to be aware of the circles in your company and strengthen the connections created within them.

5. **Encourage Cross-Functional Relationship Building:** One of the common challenges that has become more difficult is building strong cross-functional relationships. One approach that works extremely well is partnering with another function or team, even and especially one where you have a conflict. You can create an "exchange program" in which members from each other's teams are paired with a counterpart. Have them spend time together and perhaps even shadow each other for a period of time. This helps create relationships and improve the level of understanding and collaboration between your teams. Another way to facilitate relationships across the company is to set up a weekly or biweekly, fifteen- to thirty-minute conversation, where a team member meets with a different member of the team. Using this rapid-fire

approach helps to drive a deeper level of connection with significantly more people over the course of a year.

Building strong, trusting relationships is essential for every company. It is also one of the two most critical components in the personal and professional growth of every member of your team. The other is the fourth component of *The CORE Four Framework*—EXPERIENCES.

CHAPTER THIRTEEN

EXPERIENCES—Develop a Growth Skill Set

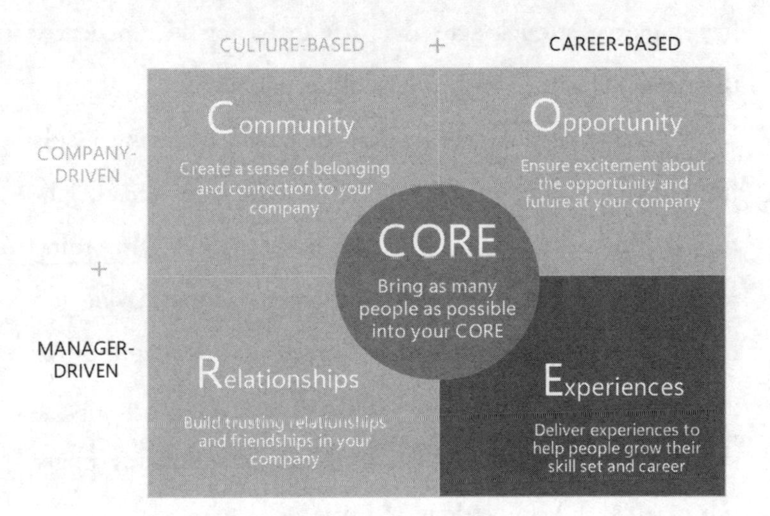

EXPERIENCE IS THE BEST tool there is to help you grow. You can study something forever, whether it is coding or cooking, but the most effective way to learn is to simply start writing code or creating in the kitchen.

In the same way, both providing and encouraging members of your team to seek growth experiences will help them feel part of the CORE of your company. Because we learn from every experience that we have, there is a need to be much more deliberate and intentional about creating specific opportunities for people. This helps someone grow their career, which in turn drives the growth of your team and company. And this is another area of risk for leaders; our survey showed that fewer than one of five employees strongly agree that they are having the experiences they need in order to grow their skill set and career.

Access to experiences are a critical factor in keeping people from leaving your company, especially in the age group of eighteen to thirty-four, where attrition is the highest. According to research by LinkedIn, the two biggest factors driving job changes for people early in their career are opportunities for growth and developing new skills.[46] Across all age groups, a stunning 94 percent of workers would stay at a company longer if it invested in helping them to learn.[47]

It is central and essential not just to create a *growth mindset* in your company, but also a *growth skill set*. The difference between the two is the willingness to take risks and try new things, over and over again.

As an example, my son and I recently decided we were going to try to learn how to make a baseball bat. Believe me, neither of us had an idea how or ability to do it. But we had our minds set on giving it a shot, so we bought a lathe, which is a wood-turning tool, and spent many hours and days making many mistakes. We could have read and thought about how to make a baseball bat forever. But by doing the work, seriously messing up, and refining our approach, we figured it out in a few weeks.

In that same spirit, we all learn throughout our lives by taking a shot at making and breaking bats. The key to developing a growth skill set is simply the willingness to continue to step to the plate over and over again, even if you swing and miss. That persistence to grab the experience is a key skill that also turns out to be exceptionally rewarding.

According to a McKinsey & Company study of over one million people in many different roles and industries, roughly 40 percent of your lifetime earnings comes from your foundational skills and what you learn in school, while the other 60 percent comes through the experience that you gain over time.[48] That experience can come from the work itself, training and development programs, and job changes that bring new experiences.

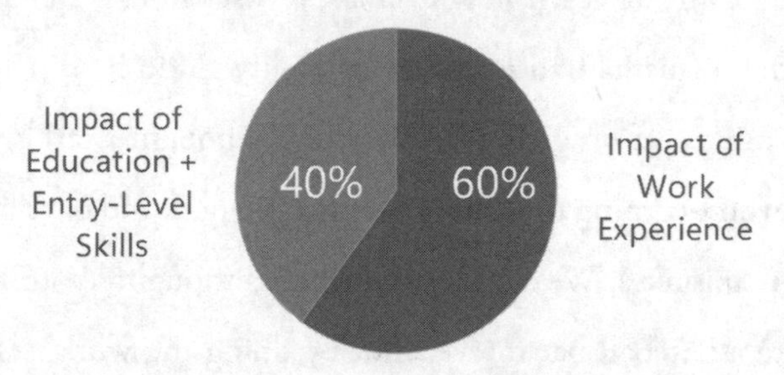

Ensuring that every member of the team has new and more experiences consistently within and across roles is mission critical for every company. One of the primary drivers behind people leaving companies or lacking motivation in their role is that they have stopped learning and growing. But leaders and managers have never been great at recognizing how critical new experiences are for members of their team until it's too late.

From a personal perspective, it's exactly the reason why I have left my last three jobs. And when I lost top performers, they consistently shared that they that felt they needed to leave to get a new experience in order to grow. That same McKinsey report highlighted that 80 percent of role changes to get experience were a new job at a new company versus making a move within their own company.

Many companies try to address this by documenting growth plans as part of their annual review process, but this is often very narrowly focused on what that team member needs to do to get their next job. It is usually not specific on the day-to-day experiences that they have to gain and how to access those opportunities. And even when these discussions happen, it's normally just a once-a-year conversation, and most lose track of those plans the day after they develop them.

One place where a growth plan isn't really needed is in software development because this plays out in a very overt way. Developers are very vocal about getting experience working on the latest technology. Even if you outsource development, the most talented coders won't want to work on an outdated platform. When you run a software company, there's no hiding from this reality as it's the most common reason why developers leave. This was such a major issue at my last company that we decided to re-platform our entire application, something that is extraordinarily hard and expensive to do for a twenty-year-old company. While we had to do this eventually, there is no question that the recruiting and retention issue accelerated our plan.

This is an extreme example of the strategic importance of

employee development. And it's exactly the way leaders now need to think. Companies need to be more intentional about baking experiences into their training and development programs and making them more accessible and available to more members of their team. Because when it comes to helping people grow, nothing is better than experience—and every experience matters.

Marbles in a Jar

Think of experiences like marbles in a jar. In your time at your company and over the course of your career, every new experience, whether it is good or bad, big or small, is another marble that you get to put in the jar. The more you grow at your company, the more fulfilling your career . . . and the fuller the jar.

Experiences Are Like Marbles in a Jar

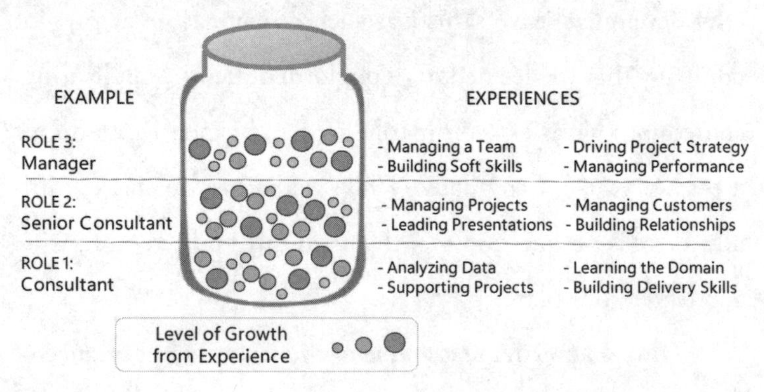

When it comes to experiences, while good ones are great, bad ones might even be better in terms of what they teach you and how they help you grow. The most difficult situations that we go through often lead to the deepest character and skill development. Shielding someone from an angry customer or a challenging project might be the worst thing you can do for them relative to their growth.

Any parent learns that when they step in to help their child, they may at the same time be stunting that child's growth. In a similar vein, while big experiences are great, small ones will help fill up that jar as well. For example, something big like leading the launch of a new product is a wonderful opportunity for anyone. But something small, like being a fly on the wall in a design meeting when a product is being developed, is also something that helps someone grow.

Perhaps the easiest way to think about or track someone's growth is to simply count the number of experiences that they are getting—the number of marbles they are putting in their jar. In that spirit, it's time to shift our thinking from delivering a traditional *training program* to instead developing an *experience plan* for every member of our team. A training program is a good tool for educating people, and it's the foundation of a *growth mindset*. In contrast, an experience plan, with a number of specific experiences laid out over time for each member of the team, can help someone create a *growth skill set*. In other words, you'll learn how to make a baseball bat by making one, not by just talking about making one.

All experiences are helpful in someone's growth. The key is to encourage members of our teams to view experiences in this way instead of narrowing everything to the next promotion. But if it's only and all about the next job for someone on your team, the good news is that they actually don't need to wait—they can get that experience right now.

If You Want the Next Job, Start Doing It Now

Early in my career, like most people, I was absolutely focused on getting the next promotion and title. That is an established pattern for all of us, and recognizing it is important. Average tenure is 1.2 years for someone aged 20 to 24, 2.6 years from 25 to 34, 4.7 years from 35 to 44, and 6.9 years from 45 to 54.[49] And frequent job switches aren't just an issue with Millennials as the average Baby Boomer switched jobs twelve times over the course of their career.[50]

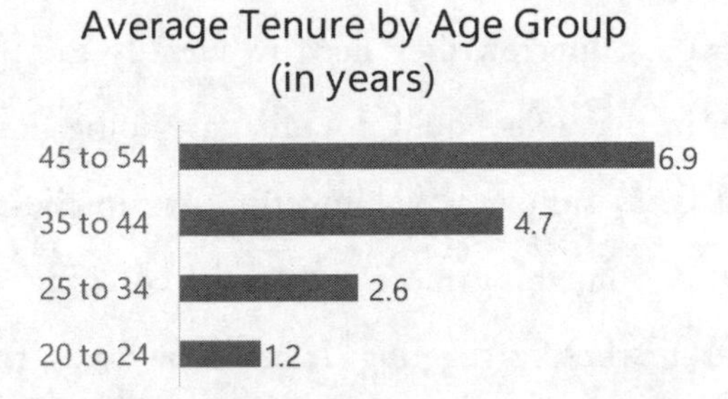

Turnover for workers turns out to be predictable, which is why it's so important for employers to be proactive. With that said, part of the ownership needs to be with the employee, and clearly communicating this is critical. There are actions that anyone can take at any company to help them move into that next role.

The best advice that I ever got to help accelerate ambition was that "if you want the next job, just start doing it now." This simple advice was a breakthrough for me. What I didn't recognize until that conversation was that I didn't have to wait. I began to understand that the role itself wasn't about the title, it was about the work you had to do and the behaviors you had to demonstrate. You didn't need someone to promote you to do either of those. You or a member of your team could begin gaining experience and having those experiences right now.

For example, if the next job someone wants is to be a manager or a director, they need to identify the things that a person in that role would do and start doing those things. It could be as simple as volunteering to run the next team meeting, or something more subtle like coaching a member of the team who is struggling. It could be doing research on competitors and briefing their team, or organizing an event for their next team outing. Each of these demonstrates that the person can do what comes next because now they have actually done the work. If someone wants to be a leader someday, they should start leading now.

I recognize that some may view it as unfair or unacceptable to do more work and not get paid for it. While I certainly understand this perspective, I respectfully disagree. The things that I have valued the most in my career have been the opportunities to gain experience. If someone was willing to give it to me, I wanted to take it. Once I understood that I didn't have to wait for someone else's permission, the floodgates opened for me. This simple shift in mindset can do the same for you and members of your team.

Over the last few years, gaining access to experiences has become more difficult. The number of people who strongly agree that they have opportunities to learn and grow has dropped by over 10 percent.[51] Ensuring folks have access to getting experience is the path to turning this around. There is a great opportunity for leaders and managers to be more intentional . . . and inspirational.

Experiences: Make Shift Happen

Here are five actions you set in motion to help encourage experiences and a growth skill set for members of your team:

1. **Develop an Experience Program for Every Position:** As we outlined earlier, we have to shift our thinking from episodic training programs to ongoing experience programs. In every role in your company, programming experiences will help people to accelerate their development and growth. In traditional programs, the output is often a test that everyone ultimately passes. Contrast this with an experience program, where the experience itself is the output. Whether it's a good or bad experience, the one thing you know is that it will help people grow. An example of a programmatic, experience-based approach that works very well in the first year for service and consulting roles

is to have the new person on the team lead a meeting or at least a portion of a presentation. It might not go well the first or even the second or third time. But that risk is limited compared to the level of learning for that individual. With that said, there is no need to limit your focus to new hires. You can also design experiences for members of your team who are moving toward manager or director roles. One example is to provide them with the experience and exposure of attending and even presenting at management meetings. Being in the "room where it happens" is an extremely powerful experience to provide for high-potential team members. So, whether it is an entry-level or a more senior-level role, defining and requiring a set of experiences within your company is something tangible that members of your team can both understand and embrace.

2. **Create an Experience Skill Set for Every Person:** While some things can be programmed across your company, it is also critical to tailor a plan to every person. Once again, think of this as getting experience doing something instead of, or in addition to, being trained on it, just like making a baseball bat. As part of your ongoing conversation with a team member, identify how they can develop

and demonstrate the skill that they want and need. This may sound really tactical, but the key is to keep a count of the new experiences that they are getting to ensure the output of the plan is tangible. Examples might include a plan where there are four separate actions: attending a sales call, taking the lead on a team meeting, working on a special project, and giving a presentation in front of a group. For that individual, each of these is a new experience and a stretch situation, which, again, is exactly where most growth occurs. Some of these might make the person feel anxious, but that can be managed. For example, if someone is nervous about presenting in front of a group, encourage them to select a topic of personal interest or expertise. This provides them with the chance to build their confidence and prepare them for tougher settings in the future. Some of the best experiences are ones that you can't put into a plan, as they will naturally occur in real time. The key is to constantly be on the lookout for team members to gain experience in taking on new things that help them grow.

3. **Enable Peer-to-Peer Exchanges:** Another incredibly effective approach is to learn from the experience of

others. When someone understands what you're going through, it's a game changer. This is where many company training programs are too high level. To be fair, most college and graduate programs also fall short. Even when they try to get real with case studies, they often lack the context of what people deal with day to day within their role. That's exactly why peer-to-peer exchanges can be so powerful. It's not the same as a Buddy System, which is more about establishing an ongoing, one-to-one relationship. A Peer-to-Peer Exchange is a process that provides people access to multiple peer-level perspectives on an ongoing basis. While some companies occasionally have peer-to-peer sessions, they aren't available consistently. In an Exchange, sessions are set in a schedule for the year at a cadence that is determined appropriate for each role. During these sessions, team members both share and learn from each other's experience to help think through and solve specific problems. Participants can submit a topic in advance, such as seeking feedback on a project or working through a difficult situation, or they can just raise topics at the beginning of each session. While it's great to learn from the experience of others, it won't happen or at least happen enough if you don't set it up as a standard process in your company.

4. **Design Shared Experiences:** One of the mistakes leaders make when they bring their entire company together is getting a big stage with bright lights and filling an agenda with talking heads. Trust me, I've done this many times, forcing people to suffer through many endless PowerPoint presentations. While this type of show may have entertained and even educated some in the past, it falls way short of the level of impact that a shared collective experience can deliver. Another mistake many of us have made is focusing on fun team-building activities as a way to build relationships. There is a place for those, but their impact is relatively limited and the effect quickly fades away. There are more creative approaches, which give people experience working on something that is meaningful and targeted to your company. One example is hosting a "hackathon" in order for people on your team to gain experience in solving a problem outside of their daily role and responsibilities. While hackathons are often associated with software development teams, this same technique can be used across the company to develop ideas, address issues, and build

collaboration in a concentrated period of time. Another idea is creating in-person or virtual customer visits to help your team members understand how your product or service is used. Having a single and simple collective experience like this can create a common language and sense of connection across your company.

5. **Encourage Experiences Every Day as Part of Your DNA:** To create a true growth skill set across the team, you need to demonstrate every day that it's part of your company's DNA. As a leader, it's important for you to encourage every team member to act on the ideas described above and then highlight and celebrate those actions across the company. One example is when someone takes the lead on a challenging customer situation that keeps getting worse or a project that falls short of hitting the mark. Focusing on how the team member took the lead and what you as a company learned creates a safe space for others to do the same. At my last company, we had someone who was sharp but inexperienced take the lead on creating a "tiger team" for customer conversions for a software upgrade. It was an extremely challenging project that ultimately fell well short of our expectations. Still, we learned a ton through

the process and wouldn't have been able to determine what to do next if we hadn't done this work. At a company-wide meeting, we highlighted the team member's leadership and the learning that we gained from this experience. And a few months later, we made sure everyone knew that he was promoted because of it. So, whether the experience goes well or falls flat, it's critical to share those stories and celebrate any experience as a growth opportunity for that individual and the company. You are sending a clear, consistent message to everyone in the company that experience matters.

One of the most powerful things you can do as a company is to set up processes and practices that help build a growth skill set for every member of your team. Ensuring that everyone has the opportunity to add another marble to their jar of experience every day is a great way to make it part of your company's DNA.

Driving the growth of every member of your team fuels the growth of your company. The path to get there is to help bring people into your inner CORE where they feel truly connected to your company, your culture, and their coworkers. *The CORE Four Framework* and practical playbook that we shared to make that shift happen is to create a sense of connection to your *community* and company culture, ensure excitement about the future long-term *opportunity*, build trusting *relationships* in your company, and deliver *experiences* that help people grow.

This is a pragmatic and proven way to hit the mark on the metric that matters the most for every leader—bringing as many people as possible into the CORE. Ensuring that every member of your team feels that this is the best job they've ever had and the best company they've ever worked for will build trust and a company that is built to last.

But having a great strategy and plan isn't enough. After all, great leaders are action figures. They make shift happen. Now it's time to get moving.

CONCLUSION
X Marks the Spot

"X marks the spot. The rest of your life begins today."

Anonymous

So now we've come to the end of our three-step journey from seeing the shift to shifting your mindset to making shift happen. As we wrap up, I wanted to share perhaps the most important tool, one that has helped me in my life and will hopefully provide you some fuel for the road ahead.

Throughout the years, I have put an "X" on blank pages and white boards to remind me of the quote "X marks the spot. The rest of your life begins today." I discovered it when I was in college and have never been able to track down who originated it. I'm still searching.

I share the quote with everyone I work with constantly. What it means to me is that anything that's happened up to this moment, both good and bad, is now officially in the past. All that matters is what you do from this point forward—from the "X" where you're standing today. For me, this simple concept has been life-altering. Like many people, I have had some really hard and tough times in my life. However, as anyone would tell you, how you deal with something is ultimately a choice.

Believe me, I say that with a deep understanding of what that actually means. Hard things are hard. Tough times are tough. Getting through these times is easier with the help of others, but ultimately, you're alone, and it's up to you.

But many people aren't stuck in the mud due to their failures but because of their accomplishments. To put it differently, they are living in the past. And their defensiveness or insecurity really stems from something that should actually be propelling them forward into the future.

With that as the thought process behind the quote, I am passing it along as a tool with the hope that it helps you recharge both personally and professionally. It's time to wipe the slate clean of both the good and the bad of your past and begin living the rest of your life today and moving forward to your future. And that's exactly what we all need to do in our lives as well as at work, because it means so much to each of us and everyone around us.

The Meaning of Work

I wrote *Holy Shift* because I feel that we all have an opportunity and responsibility to rebuild the sense of pride and purpose that comes from working on something you care about with people you care about. We've lost track of what work really means and represents on a personal level. As we think about the future of work, this concept is at the very core of the confusion and conflict that many are feeling.

Work is a word that is often misused and misunderstood. You hear phrases like "I have to go to work" or "that seems like a lot of work." The negative undertone is clear—and misplaced. What we learn over time is how extraordinarily important work can be relative to the role that it can play in our lives:

- The dignity of a job
- The energy and comfort of truly being part of a team, part of a community, and part of a company
- The feeling of support that comes from being seen, known, and valued within a group of people who care about one another
- The satisfaction that comes from accomplishing something that's really hard

- The challenge and fear of taking on something you feel like you can't do, yet being around other people who think you can
- The opportunity to leave your fingerprints on something important

The one thing we all have in common at this moment is the opportunity to shape the future of work. It starts with determining what we want our work to mean to us. A good perspective on this can be gained by considering the advice that we would give to others who are early in their career. Maybe to someone who just graduated from college, like my kids or perhaps yours.

While many would tell them to follow their *passion*, the real game changer is finding your *purpose*. Passions are transient; they come and go. What you're passionate about when you're fifteen is different from what you're passionate about when you're twenty, thirty, forty, or fifty. The point is that your interests can and will change, and there's nothing wrong with that. In fact, it's just the opposite: being open to that change is exactly what allows you to grow.

However, purpose is different from passion. For some,

their purpose might be to explore things creatively and share them with others—like an artist, entertainer, or designer. For someone else, it might be to make a difference in the lives of others—like a teacher, nurse, or social worker. Your purpose is personal. It identifies not just what we do but who we really are.

When you take away someone's work, you remove that meaning, that purpose. In some ways, you lose your identity. My dad worked until the day he died, not because he had to, but because it was part of who he was. When he had only a few weeks to live, he insisted that we bring his printer to where he was getting care so he could process invoices. His nurse confirmed that he was the first patient in the history of the hospice to have a printer set up in his room. To be clear, he wasn't a workaholic. Work at that point of his life was more like a hobby. It wasn't just what he did; it was part of who he was. And when he passed away, he left behind the example of someone whose work gave him a sense of pride and purpose. Job well done.

Now the challenge ahead for all of us is to find that same space. That's the heart of the matter and what matters most.

CONCLUSION: X Marks the Spot

I hope what I have shared helps you to create a *Holy Shift* for you and those around you. This is truly the opportunity of a lifetime for all of us to do just that.

It's time to start over and begin again.

It's time to move *forward.*

"X" marks the spot.

Resources

Playbook to Shift Your Mindset

MINDSET SHIFT #1 Shift from Treating Culture as a Tactic to Going After It as a Strategy	1. Ensure the Leadership Team Owns Culture 2. Set Stretch Targets with a Proactive Push 3. Create a Strategic Framework 4. Clearly Communicate with Candor 5. Adapt and Adjust
MINDSET SHIFT #2 Pivot from Bring Back *(Move Backward)* to Bring Together *(Move Forward)*	1. Refocus Your Strategy 2. Create a Comprehensive Plan 3. Make Your Approach Crystal Clear 4. Invest in Bringing People Together 5. Change the Narrative
MINDSET SHIFT #3 Migrate from Macro *(Our Company)* to Micro *(Me and My Circle)*	1. Resource and Empower Teams 2. Methodically Mentor Managers 3. Focus on Strengthening Someone's Circle 4. Focus on Level of Impact 5. Understand and Improve Individual Experience
MINDSET SHIFT #4 Move from Managing *(You Work for Me)* to Coaching *(We Work Together)*	1. Provide Guidance, Not Direction 2. Focus on Superpower Skills 3. Encourage Self-Awareness and Growth 4. Provide Greater Autonomy and Ownership 5. Provide Real-Time Feedback
MINDSET SHIFT #5 Evolve from Evaluation *(Confrontation)* to Conversation *(Collaboration)*	1. Create Coaching Conversations 2. Simplify Performance Process 3. Separate Performance, Compensation, and Career Conversations 4. Create an Expectation of Collaboration 5. Instill Pride and Drive Progress

"The CORE Four Framework" for Moving Your Company Foreword

Culture-Based CORE Model Components: *Community and Relationships*	Career-Based CORE Model Components: *Opportunity and Experiences*
The goal is to build a sense of connection to your company by ensuring people feel a sense of belonging and helping them to build trusting relationships with others on the team.	The objective is to help build someone's individual career by providing clarity about future opportunities and experiences that help them to grow.

Company-Driven CORE Model Components: *Community and Opportunity*	Manager-Driven CORE Model Components: *Relationships and Experiences*
The company owns putting the right processes, systems, and structures in place, which build a sense of community and ensure people understand their future opportunities.	The manager owns helping team members build connections and relationships as well as ensuring that they have experiences that help them grow.

Resources

Your Practical Playbook for Making Shift Happen

CORE PLAY #1 COMMUNITY Drive Connection to Company and Culture	1. Drive Connection with Your Campus 2. Host Management Collaboration Weeks 3. Create Cohorts 4. Invest in Company Retreats and Events 5. Conduct a Vision, Mission, and Values Workout
CORE PLAY #2 OPPORTUNITY Ensure Excitement about the Future	1. Consider Career Lattices 2. Encourage Lateral Career Moves 3. Create a Development Plan for Each Team Member 4. Leverage a Rolling Approach for Individual Goals 5. Create a Process to Showcase and Recognize Employees
CORE PLAY #3 RELATIONSHIPS Build Trust and Strengthen Teams	1. Create a Buddy System 2. Get Personal 3. Level Up Your One-on-One 4. Create Common Connections 5. Encourage Cross-Functional Relationship Building
CORE PLAY #4 EXPERIENCES Develop a Growth Skill Set	1. Develop an Experience Program for Every Position 2. Create an Experience Skill Set for Every Person 3. Enable Peer-to-Peer Exchanges 4. Design Shared Experiences 5. Encourage Experiences Every Day as Part of Your DNA

Acknowledgments

EVERYTHING IN THIS BOOK is something that I learned from or because of somebody else. All of the ideas came from *communities* I've been part of, *opportunities* I've been given, *relationships* I've built, and *experiences* I've had. Those are four things that are at the CORE of any and every career. My hope is that passing along the many lessons I've learned along the way will help you on your journey. In that spirit, there are many people to thank.

I'll start with the three most important people in my life. My amazing wife, Kim, for being the love of my life and my partner for over thirty years, helping me to try to become the best version of myself. My wonderful daughter, Emma, and son, Ian, for being the inspiration in my life. I could have written this entire book just about how lucky I am to be their dad.

To my mom and dad for being my role models and

setting an example of what it means to wake up every day and go to work with a sense of purpose. They always believed in me, even when there was no evidence that they should. And to my rockstar sister, Lisa, for always having my back and being so supportive. The journey outlined at the beginning of this book is one that we shared together.

On a cold, rainy day, I shared the firehose of ideas that led to this book with Glen Tullman. His reaction in that moment—his excitement—made me believe in myself. That's what great mentors and great friends do . . . and he did and continues to do for me and so many others. But I have been so lucky to have many incredible mentors along the way, including Scott Sonkin, Andy Absler, Ken Aran, Neil Hunn, Matt Likens, Lee Shapiro, and Joe Carey, whom we all miss dearly. He was in my thoughts constantly while I wrote this book, both laughing with me and encouraging me at the same time.

To my many friends who generously stepped in to help review *Holy Shift*, providing incredibly helpful edits and suggestions, including Diane Adams, Michael Alter, Michael Kraut, Bryan Schwartz, Craige Stout, Brian Vandenberg, and Kevin Weinstein. Their ideas and observations helped turn this book into one of real substance.

A special shout-out to Tom Scanlan, my partner at InCommon, for being the first person to jump in and join me on this journey to turn an idea into a company. What we've now created has the potential to make a real difference. Exciting stuff . . . more to come.

And to our wonderful team from my ten years at Strata, including the many leaders along the way whom I learned so much from: John Martino, Steve Lefar, Martin Luethi, Liz Kirk, Jennifer Rauworth, Tushar Pandey, Vince Panozzo, Frank Stevens, Cara Boaz, Christie Markiewicz, Scott Schoenknecht, Joel Gerber, Brian Groves, Alina Henderson, John Baker, Tushar Patel, and Dan Vergauwen. I would like to add a very special shout-out to Heidi Farrell and Dan Van De Voorde, our truly incredible leaders on our people operations and human resources team whom I had the opportunity to partner with and learn so much from. They were the ones who truly made the magic happen.

I was fortunate to have the opportunity to work with Jennifer Gingerich, Billie Brownell, Justin Batt, and the collective team at Forefront Books and Simon & Schuster. They provided incredibly helpful guidance in this process. A special thank-you to Phil Newman for his editorial assistance. This was my first time writing a book on my own, so I had many questions and a lot to learn. The entire team was very patient and supportive along the way.

A special shout-out to my cohort and forum of friends Arsen Avakian, Jason Beans, Clint Coghill, Ryan Ruskin, Ed Scanlan, J Schwan, and Steve Traxler. I have learned so much about what it means to be a leader and friend from each of you. I tried my best to pass along those lessons in this book. We all miss our friend Eric Cohen, but his presence is absolutely still with us. His was the voice of reason in my head as I wrote *Holy Shift.* I did my best to capture his spirit in the story that I shared.

And finally, as an apology to the many people who I missed mentioning, I just wanted to end where I began. While I am incredibly appreciative of the many *communities*, *opportunities, relationships*, and *experiences* that I've been part of, everything that I outlined in this book only happened because of the many people who stepped in and stepped up along the way. I've been incredibly fortunate to have been around so many people I've learned so much from.

We all have that same opportunity to share what we learn to help *make shift happen* in the lives of others. "X" marks the spot; that journey begins today.

Notes

1. "The Essence of Leadership with Randall Stutman," posted 10 November 2020, The Knowledge Project Podcast, YouTube channel, https://youtu.be/b_norXr5dR0?t=290.

2. Charles Hirschman and Elizabeth Mogford, "Immigration and the American Industrial Revolution From 1880 to 1920," National Library of Medicine, 1 December 2009, https://doi.org/10.1016/j.ssresearch.2009.04.001.

3. Carl Zimmer, "Did the Black Death Really Kill Half of Europe? New Research Says No," *New York Times*, 10 February 2022 https://www.nytimes.com/2022/02/10/science/black-death.html; and "Black Death: pandemic, medieval Europe," Britannica, last updated 11 April 2023, https://www.britannica.com/event/Black-Death.

4. Christine R. Johnson, "How the Black Death Made Life Better," Washington University in St. Louis, Department of History, 18 June 2021, https://history.wustl.edu/news/how-black-death-made-life-better.

5. Bill Palmer, "Our 1918 Pandemic—the Numbers Then and Now," *The Marshall Independent*, 27 March 2021, https://www.marshallindependent.com/opinion/local-columns/2021/03/our-1918-pandemic-the-numbers-then-and-now/; and "1918 Pandemic (H1N1 virus)," Centers for Disease Control and Prevention, last reviewed 20 March 2019, https://www.cdc.gov/flu/pandemic-resources/1918-pandemic-h1n1.html.

6. Aaron O'Neill, "Increase in Hourly Wages in the US during the Spanish Flu Pandemic 1900–1928," Statista, 21 June 2022, https://www.statista.com/statistics/1103413/us-wages-spanish-flu/.

7. "How the Devastating 1918 Flu Pandemic Helped Advance US Women's Rights," The Conversation, 1 March 2018, https://theconversation.com/how-the-devastating-1918-flu-pandemic-helped-advance-us-womens-rights-91045.

8. *CEOs Driving Growth: The Workplace Redefined*, Global Pulse Survey by YPO and InCommon, November 2022.

9. Franz Kafka, *Metamorphosis* (1915; London: Penguin Classics, 1995).

10. Phillippa Lally et al, "How Are Habits Formed: Modelling Habit Formation in the Real World," *European Journal of Social Psychology*, 2010: 40, 998–1009, https://citeseerx.ist.psu.edu/viewdoc/download?doi=10.1.1.695.830&rep=rep1&type=pdf.

11. "Majority of Employees Prefer Remote or Hybrid Work Despite Feeling Disconnected," 2022 Global Benefits Attitudes Survey, WTW, https://www.wtwco.com/en-US/Insights/2022/04/majority-of-employees-prefer-remote-or-hybrid-work-despite-feeling-disconnected.

12. Raheel Mushtaq et al, "Relationship Between Loneliness, Psychiatric Disorders and Physical Health? A Review on the Psychological Aspects of Loneliness," *Journal of Clinical and Diagnostic Research,* 8, no. 9, 20 September 2014, https:doi.org/10.7860/JCDR/2014/10077.4828.

13. "Striving for Balance, Advocating for Change," The Deloitte Global 2022 Gen Z & Millennial Survey, https://www2.deloitte.com/content/dam/Deloitte/cn/Documents/about-deloitte/deloitte-2022-genz-millennial-survey-en-220601.pdf.

14. "Adapt to Work Everywhere: What the Great Resignation Can Teach Us about Employee Priorities," Topia, 2022, https://www.topia.com/wp-content/uploads/2022/03/Topia-Adapt-2022.pdf.

15. "Workers place greater importance on flexible or remote work options," in Lane Gillespie, "Survey: 56% of Workers Plan to Look for a Job in the Next 12 Months," Bankrate, 3 April 2023, https://www.bankrate.com/personal-finance/job-seekers-survey/.

16. Andrés Tapia, "Return to Office: The Moment of Truth?" Korn Ferry, accessed 12 June 2023, https://www.kornferry.com/insights/this-week-in-leadership/return-to-office-the-moment-of-truth.

17. "The Flex Report," Flex Index, https://www.flex.scoopforwork.com/stats-report.

18. Ray A. Smith, "Quiet Quitters Make Up Half the U.S. Workforce, Gallup Says," *Wall Street Journal*, updated 29 September 2022, https://www.wsj.com/articles/quiet-quitters-make-up-half-the-u-s-workforce-gallup-says-11662517806.

19. Jim Harter, "Is Quiet Quitting Real?" Gallup, 6 September 2022, https://www.gallup.com/workplace/398306/quiet-quitting-real.aspx.

20. Todd Bishop, "Microsoft Unveils 'Viva' on Teams in Bid to Shake up $300B Employee Experience Technology Market," GeekWire, 4 February 2021, https://www.geekwire.com/2021/microsoft-unveils-viva-teams-bid-shake-300b-employee-experience-technology-market/.

21. Indicators: Leadership & Management, "Employee Trust in Organizational Leadership," Gallup, https://www.gallup.com/404252/indicator-leadership-management.aspx.

22. Naina Dhingra et al, "Help Your Employees Find Purpose—or

Watch Them Leave," McKinsey & Co., 5 April 2021, https://www.mckinsey.com/capabilities/people-and-organizational-performance/our-insights/help-your-employees-find-purpose-or-watch-them-leave.

23. Kim Parker, "About a Third of U.S. Workers Who Can Work from Home Now Do So All the Time," Pew Research Center, 30 March 2023, https://www.pewresearch.org/fact-tank/2023/03/30/about-a-third-of-us-workers-who-can-work-from-home-do-so-all-the-time/.

24. Rob Cross and Peter Gray, "Optimizing Return-to-Office Strategies With Organizational Network Analysis," MITSloan Management Review, 29 June 2021, https://sloanreview.mit.edu/article/optimizing-return-to-office-strategies-with-organizational-network-analysis/.

25. "What Is Employee Engagement and How Do You Improve It?" Gallup, accessed 12 June 2023, https://www.gallup.com/workplace/285674/improve-employee-engagement-workplace.aspx.

26. "Mental Health at Work: Managers and Money," Workforce Institute, https://www.ukg.com/resources/article/mental-health-work-managers-and-money.

27. Indicators: Leadership & Management, Gallup.

28. "Performance Review Peril: Adobe Study Shows Office Workers Waste Time and Tears," Adobe, 11 January 2017, https://news.adobe.com/news/news-details/2017/Performance-Review-Peril-Adobe-Study-Shows-Office-Workers-Waste-Time-and-Tears/default.aspx.

29. Indicators: Leadership & Management, Gallup.

30. "What Is Employee Engagement and How Do You Improve It?" Gallup.

31. "Performance Review Peril," Adobe.

Notes

32. Jim Harter, "Is Quiet Quitting Real?" Gallup.

33. InCommon Survey of U.S. Workers Across 15 Industrial Sectors and Every Region of the Country, 2023.

34. "Evergreen," *Merriam-Webster*, 2023, https://www.merriam-webster.com/dictionary/evergreen.

35. Hoag Levins, "William Kissick and The Iron Triangle of Health Economics: A Policy Expert Who Played a Key Role in Shaping LDI," Penn LDI, 5 October 2016, https://ldi.upenn.edu/our-work/research-updates/william-kissick-and-the-iron-triangle-of-health-economics/.

36. "Expectations at Work: How Changing Employee Expectations Are Impacting Talent Attraction and Retention," BCW Change, https://www.bcw-global.com/assets/BCW-Expectations-At-Work-Study-2022.pdf.

37. "Community," *Merriam-Webster*, 2023, https://www.merriam-webster.com/dictionary/community.

38. Deanna deBara, "Top Findings from Lattice's Career Progression Survey," Lattice, 13 September 2021, https://lattice.com/library/top-findings-from-lattices-career-progression-survey.

39. Lori Li, "17 Surprising Statistics about Employee Retention," TINYpulse by Limeade, 8 April 2022, https://www.tinypulse.com/blog/17-surprising-statistics-about-employee-retention.

40. *The American Upskilling Study: Empowering Workers for the Jobs of Tomorrow*, Gallup, June 2021, https://www.gallup.com/analytics/354374/the-american-upskilling-study.aspx.

41. "Building the Agile Future," *2023 Workplace Learning Report,* LinkedIn Learning, https://learning.linkedin.com/content/dam/me/learning/en-us/pdfs/workplace-learning-report/LinkedIn-Learning_Workplace-Learning-Report-2023-EN.pdf.

42. Alok Patel and Stephanie Plowman, "The Increasing Importance of a Best Friend at Work," Gallup, 17 August 2022, https://www.gallup.com/workplace/397058/increasing-importance-best-friend-work.aspx.

43. Karen A. Jehn and Priti Pradhan Shah, "Interpersonal Relationships and Task Performance: An Examination of Mediation Processes in Friendship and Acquaintance Groups," Psycnet, *Journal of Personality and Social Psychology* 72, no. 4, (1997): 775–790, https://psycnet.apa.org/fulltext/1997-03701-006.pdf?auth_token=dd3d02ae3974bec314ada83086d7bec34520fde5.

44. Robert Waldinger and Marc Schulz, "What the Longest Study on Human Happiness Found Is the Key to a Good Life," *The Atlantic*, 19 January 2023, https://www.theatlantic.com/ideas/archive/2023/01/harvard-happiness-study-relationships/672753/.

45. Dawn Klinghoffer, Candice Young, and Dave Haspas, "Every New Employee Needs an Onboarding 'Buddy,'" *Harvard Business Review*, 6 June 2019, https://hbr.org/2019/06/every-new-employee-needs-an-onboarding-buddy.

46. "Building the Agile Future," 2023 *Workplace Learning Report,* LinkedIn Learning.

47. Abigail Johnson Hess, "LinkedIn: 94% of Employees Say They Would Stay at a Company Longer for This Reason—and It's Not a Raise," CNBC, 27 February 2019, https://www.cnbc.com/2019/02/27/94percent-of-employees-would-stay-at-a-company-for-this-one-reason.html.

48. Anu Madgavkar et al, "Human Capital at Work: The Value of Experience," McKinsey & Co., 2 June 2022, https://www.mckinsey.com/capabilities/people-and-organizational-performance/our-insights/human-capital-at-work-the-value-of-experience#/.

49. "Table 1. Median Years of Tenure with Current Employer for Employed Wage and Salary Workers by Age and Sex, Selected Years, 2012-2022," U.S. Bureau of Labor Statistics, modified 22 September 2022, https://www.bls.gov/news.release/tenure.t01.htm.

50. "Number of Jobs, Labor Market Experience, Marital Status, and Health: Results from a National Longitudinal Survey," Bureau of Labor Statistics, US Department of Labor, 31 August 2021, https://www.bls.gov/news.release/pdf/nlsoy.pdf.

51. Jim Harter, "Is Quiet Quitting Real?" Gallup.

About the Author

DAN MICHELSON is the Founder and CEO of InCommon, a *for-purpose* company that helps companies turn culture into a strategy that drives productivity and engagement by ensuring everyone feels connected and part of the CORE. His expertise is in building high-performing, high-growth companies.

For the prior 10 years he was CEO of Strata, a 500-person healthcare technology company with a mission to *help heal healthcare*. Strata was recognized as one of the nation's fastest-growing companies, one of the best places to work, and had the highest customer satisfaction in the industry. In his time with Strata, the valuation of the company increased by more than $1 billion. Prior to joining Strata, Dan spent a decade as the Chief Marketing Officer and Chief Strategy Officer of Allscripts, helping the company grow from 100 to over 6,000 employees and over $1 billion in annual revenue. In both companies, culture and connection was the center of the strategy.

About the Author

Dan's personal mission is to help people, companies, and communities grow. He is an Adjunct Professor at the Quinlan School of Business at Loyola University in Chicago. Dan is also the Founder of projectMUSIC, a benefit concert that sends children in need to overnight camp, and of HackHunger, a collaborative of tech companies working to crack the code on hunger.

Dan earned his bachelor's in finance from Indiana University and an MBA from DePaul University. He is an avid runner, having completed twenty marathons as well as an Ironman Triathlon. Dan and his wife, Kim, have two children, Emma and Ian.

TheHolyShift.com